# FIX YOUR
# DOG
## IN THREE EASY STEPS

# FIX YOUR
# DOG
## IN THREE EASY STEPS

BE YOUR OWN DOG BEHAVIOURIST

## LEON TOWERS

First published in Great Britain in 2024 by Cassell, an imprint of
Octopus Publishing Group Ltd
Carmelite House
50 Victoria Embankment
London EC4Y 0DZ
www.octopusbooks.co.uk

An Hachette UK Company
www.hachette.co.uk

Distributed in the US by
Hachette Book Group
1290 Avenue of the Americas
4th and 5th Floors
New York, NY 10104

Distributed in Canada by
Canadian Manda Group
664 Annette St.
Toronto, Ontario, Canada M6S 2C8

ISBN 978-1-78840-500-3

A CIP catalogue record for this book is available from the British Library.

Printed and bound in Great Britain.

Typeset in 11.25/16pt Heldane Text by Jouve (UK), Milton Keynes

13 5 7 9 10 8 6 4 2

This FSC® label means that materials used for the product have been responsibly sourced.

Disclaimer:
This book is intended to give general guidance on the care and training of dogs. It is not a substitute
for tailored professional advice. We recommend that you consult a veterinarian or other professional if
your dog has any specific health concerns or dietary needs. The author and publisher disclaim
any liability directly or indirectly from the use of the information in this book by any person.

I dedicate this book to the three true loves of my life:
Scooby, gone but never forgotten
My mum, Audrey Towers
My twin flame, Dean Bailey

# CONTENTS

## Part 3: Final Thoughts

# INTRODUCTION

Hi, I'm Leon Towers. I'm a qualified dog psychologist, behaviourist, canine nutritionist and hydrotherapist. In the last 15 years I've fixed the behaviour and fitness of over 16,500 dogs. YES, REALLY. And improved the lives of their owners using only the POWER OF THREE and positive reinforcement. And now I'm SO excited to share everything I know about dogs with YOU to give you the confidence to manage your dog's problem behaviour.

Whether your dog is a frisky minx who just won't stop humping or a shaking nervous wreck with separation anxiety, whether he's the canine equivalent of a wrecking ball or a loose cannon on the lead, I want to EMPOWER you to be able to understand and fix him. Because once you understand the basics of training and how simple it is to follow my techniques without fancy words or difficult methods, you'll be set for life.

This stress-free guide will give you a personalized, easy-to-follow training plan to fix any doggy dilemma in THREE easy steps.

### Not your average dog trainer

In my opinion, dog training books are all the same. BORING! They use outdated methods from 90 years ago. YAWN.

This book is different. And this book works!

I don't LOOK like a dog behaviourist (I'm more skinny jeans and tattoos than tweed and red trousers), and I don't TALK like a dog behaviourist (no plummy vowels here, thank you very much, I call a spade a SPADE). But I can assure you that I am one!

You might have seen me on TV – *Embarrassing Pets, Crufts, Meet the PAW-rents: Celebs and Their Dogs,* and *My Gay Dog and Other Animals* – where I'm the tall, tattooed, talkative 'expert'. I don't follow what everyone else says and I've never been backwards at coming forwards, I can tell you! I'm surrounded by dogs 24/7 in my doggy day care, The Lodge, which I run with my partner Dean. We have between 12 and 20 dogs in our care every day and I learn so much seeing them interact and TALK DOG to each other.

Old-school dog training is complicated – whistle training, clicker training – it makes my head hurt! I avoid those things because I want you to understand in an EASY way. I don't want to bog you down with complicated things that make you feel rubbish when they don't work. I want to empower you to fix your own dog without the endless interruptions of all these dos and don'ts and contradictory things. I want it to be easy, three steps and BOOM. Done.

## The POWER OF THREE

Though every issue might seem like a one-off – the rogue that forgets his recall when it's time to go home, the doggy diva that tap dances on your dining room table, the anxiety-ridden pup that rips the carpet up – the fix will ALWAYS come down to at least one of THREE simple things.

1. DIET
2. ENVIRONMENT
3. MENTAL STIMULATION

We look at all three of these factors in more detail in Chapter 3. Forget complex methods and ten-step techniques, this is all about keeping it simple and practical so YOU can do it at home.

It's important to say, before we begin, that with any behavioural issue, always get your dog checked over by a vet to make sure that they're not in pain or that they don't have underlying reasons for their unwanted behaviour. For example, if your dog is terrified of loud sounds, they could have an ear infection, if they're banging into things, they could have something wrong with their eyes, or if they're licking their privates, they might have a yeast infection.

## Whatever your dog's issue, we can fix it

I can't tell you how many times I've fixed a dog that owners have been told is UNTREATABLE by other trainers. Ridiculous! But whether you've got a rescue dog that needs help settling into his new environment, an anti-social pooch that needs to learn how to TALK DOG to his peers, or you're welcoming a new puppy into your family home and want some advice on how to train him in healthy behaviours, I've got you covered. Because the truth is, it's not really the DOG that needs training, it's usually the OWNER. And I know you want to fix your dog because you've picked up this book, so you're already halfway there.

In Part 2, I'm going to give you the benefit of my 1-to-1 private sessions through a series of case studies looking at EVERY possible issue you might have with your dog from obedience to toilet training. Some of the dogs in the book are extreme cases but I want to show you that no matter your dog's issue, there will ALWAYS be a fix.

You'll see how I investigate the root cause of the dog's challenge as I grill the owners on when the problems started and what they've done to try to solve them. DIG DIG DIG. It's like therapy for the owner. I love it when I see the 'penny drop' expression on their face. I know I've connected the dots and they get it.

## How to use this book

It doesn't matter how old your dog is, how long you've had him, or when the behaviour started. With my training tips YOU CAN fix any issue with your dog.

I want you to think of this book as a handy resource, like having me – all six foot two of me – in your pocket to call on whenever you need me. Get your mind out of the gutter Sandra, this is about dogs! Feel free to dip in and out as issues arise and use it as your dog's LIFE MANUAL. I'll always be here to help with an easy fix and a cheeky quip so you and your dog can enjoy one another and grow a great partnership built on mutual TRUST AND RESPECT. I use only positive reinforcement – no fear, force or bullying.

I ask you to come to this book, and to other dog owners, with NO JUDGEMENT. We all do it. That inner bitchy voice pipes up. We hear about someone not walking their dog and we say, 'That's disgusting.' Or we see a dog wearing a muzzle and we go, 'He looks vicious, better stay away.' What I hope the case studies in Part 2 will show is that there are *multiple* valid reasons for all these things. So, please, hold off your judgement. That dog not being walked might have pulled their owner over or the dog wearing the muzzle might be in training or a danger to himself because he eats anything and everything. You just don't know.

We're going to break down the theory, squash the age-old myths and look at real-life case studies to give you LASTING results.

This is the first training book for dogs that will help fix your dog AND make you laugh at the same time. So, strap yourself in, because I'm going to blow your mind with how easy it is to FIX YOUR DOG.

# Part 1: Understanding Dogs

## Getting to know you

In this section, we explore the basics of dog behaviour and psychology, from how dogs communicate to their ability to learn, so that we can better understand our dogs. Park everything you think you know about dogs and listen up. I'm going to BLOW YOUR MIND.

Over the next seven chapters, I'll look at everything from nutrition, environment and mental stimulation to basic training principles and how to set your own training goals. We'll delve into the essential parts of dog ownership so you can lay the foundations for good behaviour, learning effective techniques to communicate and bond with your dog.

If we understand what truly makes dogs TICK, what they want from us, what they need from us, we can create a better partnership with them for LIFE.

# CHAPTER 1

# THE DOG'S VOICE

My journey to becoming a dog trainer hasn't been a regular one. It seems more like a series of connected events that led me here. Experiences good and downright AWFUL that have given me a unique understanding of dogs, how they think and why they behave the way they do.

I didn't grow up around dogs. There was no family pet because, to be honest, there was no *family*. My dad died when I was a baby and the police thought my mum had killed him. He'd actually killed himself. But I was taken into care and lost contact with my birth mum, Audrey.

I lived with different foster carers; some were great, some were truly awful. Social services only checked on me twice in all those years and when I told them what was happening with the bad foster parents, I was dismissed as having an overactive imagination. It was DEVASTATING to know that no one would listen to me or believe me. I had no VOICE.

Little did I know that my childhood experiences would give me a UNIQUE understanding of dogs and set me up for my career as a dog trainer because dogs don't have voices either. They can't let you know why they're reacting a certain way. If a dog is in pain, they can't *tell* you, but they can be aggressive, guarding the pain. I totally understand that feeling. Every single thing I learned back then gave me the tools to do the job I do today.

Now I am THE DOGS' VOICE because they don't have an advocate or someone sticking up for them. Most of the time, dogs get blamed for behaviour that their owners have caused. And I call people out for it. I tell them *they've* caused the issue, not the dog.

## Healing through hydrotherapy

Having survived my childhood and time as a runaway teen, I was desperate to help other people like me. As an adult, I've had HUNDREDS of jobs – from restaurants and retail to TV presenting and being in a boy band – but in my thirties, with kids of my own, I worked with autistic children and young adults in a residential unit and fostered 12 children, giving them the security and stability that I never had. Doing that work was really rewarding and helped heal a part of me. It also taught me so much.

Then one day I had MY LIGHTBULB MOMENT.

Our last foster child had moved out and I was left with a massive void. I was watching TV, feeling like I had no purpose, and this documentary about hydrotherapy started where they were rehabilitating a dog who had a spinal injury that meant it couldn't move its back legs. Up to that point, I had NEVER sat through 90 minutes of ANYTHING but I watched this *entire* documentary on the edge of my seat. I was MESMERIZED.

My head was buzzing. What WAS that? I got straight onto my laptop and began researching hydrotherapy for dogs and what qualifications you needed. How did it work? How did you set up a pool? I spent hours and hours trawling the internet. If I was going to do this, I wanted a qualification because I didn't have a qualification in ANYTHING. I'd left school at 14.

I finally found a rehabilitation centre, called Greyfriars, set up by Angela Griffiths. She founded the National Association of Registered Canine Hydrotherapists (NARCH) and travels the world teaching hydrotherapy. If I was doing this, I wanted to do it there. They're simply the BEST. At this stage, I didn't even know the structure of a dog – obviously I knew the tail, the paws and the face but HOW would I do a course like this? Eventually my curiosity got the better of me and I thought, 'What have I got to lose?' I signed up before I could change my mind.

They sent me a welcome pack with a diagram of every single part of the dog. There were HUNDREDS of words I didn't know – CRUCIATE, LIGAMENT, WHAT? I panicked. I didn't think I'd be able to do it.

That self-doubt that had been put into my head as a child, constantly being told I was no good at anything and that I'd amount to nothing, was back. I got PURE ANXIETY. But I didn't quit, I sat there 14 hours a day and studied that skeleton and I read all the information in the pack. I learned the anatomy, the muscles, the brain, the spine, all the veterinary terminology.

When I turned up for my first seminar, I was the class swot putting my hand up for every answer. It turned out they hadn't expected us to learn it ALL before we started. But I'd been so excited and keen that I'd memorized the whole thing.

My very first hydrotherapy case study as a trainee was a greyhound who needed to build up muscle. I was *so* nervous, stepping into the warm water and getting into the big treadmill but all my fears disappeared as I lifted the dog's two back paws to help her to walk. It was like MAGIC. I was making a *difference*. It still makes me so emotional to remember that day. It was a LIFE-CHANGING MOMENT.

My second case study was a Rottweiler. The big boss Angela was supervising with a stern face and I remember that as I put my hands on the dog, she somehow communicated to me that she was in pain and I asked the owner why she wasn't on any pain medication. She told me she thought it was a cop-out.

I LOST IT! I said, 'This dog is in AGONY. Get her onto some pain relief as soon as you leave here.' I heard all the other trainee hydrotherapists gasp. I'd only been in the treadmill twice. I hadn't even got my qualification and I'd kicked off at a client. Angela's face was like thunder as she said, 'Can I have a word?' I thought, that's it. I'm out. She took me to the side and told me, 'I have NEVER in 25 years seen what happened there happen. You are going to be an amazing hydrotherapist. The fact that you were outspoken and went with conviction without even thinking about it shows me you're putting the *dog* first.'

After she said that, I FLEW! I absorbed all her advice and praise like a sponge. I passed EVERY SINGLE essay, exam and practical. It was like having a superpower. It just blew me away. Angela was one of the first people to BELIEVE in me and give me praise. And it was hard earned.

## A daily dose of dog

Once I had my qualification, I decided to start my own business. So in 2009, I set up a doggy day care with a five-star luxury hotel for dogs – The House of Hugo – with a hydrotherapy swimming pool. The whole place was 1,850 square metres (20,000 square feet). HUGE. I couldn't get a bank loan so I got 22 credit cards with £1,000 of credit on one, £2,000 on another, £4,000 on another until I had £36,000 and I drew out the credit in cash and I bought the pool. I look back now and wonder HOW THE HELL I did it. It was such a massive thing to do with no guarantee of success but I had this self-belief because of Angela. It never even came into my head that it wasn't going to work. People were asking me what Plan B was and I told them, 'Plan B is Plan A.' End of. I didn't question it at all.

We were so busy. We were doing 70 swims a week in the pool and I was seeing so many dogs up close and personal on a daily basis that I got an intense understanding of what makes them tick, how they interact with each other, how they learn, how they TALK. In many ways it was the making of me but it took me a loooong time to pay back all the debt. I still owed thousands when I closed the business. We had a one-way mirror so we could study them interacting. That's insight that many people never get. I wasn't purposefully studying them; it was natural and organic.

I ran the day care for seven years and did hydrotherapy for places like Dog's Trust, for 'problem dogs' that couldn't be rehomed. Having an hour's swim each week brought down their stress levels to the point where they could be rehomed. It was like walking into magic water. The dogs came out changed and so did I.

And then I fell in love.

## Scooby, my first love

We all remember our first love. That whirlwind of emotions, pure joy, and finally feeling like you're HOME. And that's how it was with Scooby. My first dog. My first LOVE. Being brought up in the care system, I never understood the true meaning of unconditional love. He taught me that. He didn't blame me for anything and there was no nastiness in him.

I got Scooby, an Airedale Terrier, who looked like a big ball of fluff, when I was 30 and he was 8 weeks old. Back then I didn't know ANYTHING about dog training. He was really cheeky, bouncy and full of attitude. A BIG personality. Remind you of anyone?!

I FELL IN LOVE.

Scooby loved chasing balls. I used to walk around with pound coins in my pocket to reimburse people when he stole their tennis ball. One time we were at the beach and he STOLE a ball out of someone's car. I have NO IDEA how he knew there was a ball in this man's car but it was mortifying. The first I knew of it was this man SCREAMING as Scooby scarpered down the beach with the ball. There was no way I was getting it off him!

He was so naughty. He loved muddy puddles. I would try to drag him away but every time he would SLUT DROP into the mud, rolling around in it. He'd eyeball me before he did it as if to say WATCH THIS DAD! Another time, he rolled in a fox carcass. Absolutely stinking.

But God, I loved him.

We had seven amazing years together but when Scooby died, it almost killed me. I talk about losing your dog, and my experiences with it, in Chapter 29. It's something no one can prepare you for but hopefully my journey will help other people. I haven't been able to have another dog of my own since Scooby. The dogs I train and look after at the day care are my substitute dogs for now.

# CHAPTER 2

# RETRAIN YOUR BRAIN

It's time to rethink EVERYTHING you know about dogs. Humans have misunderstood dogs for decades. These old training techniques haven't evolved with the times or the roles that dogs now play in our lives. Ninety years ago, the role of dogs was TOTALLY different. We didn't have that bond that we have today. Dogs were mainly used for working or security. It's only recently that we've realized how special and intelligent dogs are. How they can change a person's life. When you think of how child-rearing books have changed in the last 30–40 years, it's surprising that dog manuals are still STUCK IN THE PAST. They don't work. I hate the mentality, 'We've always done it this way.' Nothing can move forward or evolve with that attitude.

## The myth of pack theory

The most damaging advice, which is still used by lots of trainers and organizations, is PACK THEORY or dominance theory. It's the root of most traditional dog advice and stems from a study of CAPTIVE WOLVES in the 1940s. A scientist called Rudolph Schenkel noted that there was an ALPHA dog in each pack and that this position was achieved through dominance and bullying. This idea of pack hierarchy and dominance was taken up in the 1960s by scientist and wolf researcher Dr David Mech and in 1970 he published his bestselling book, *The Wolf: Ecology and Behavior of an Endangered Species*.

Although the book was about wolves, the dog training world latched on to this idea that to successfully train your *dog* you had to DOMINATE it to show it who was boss. There was a pecking order and YOU the human had to be at the top of it. YOU had to become the Alpha. This meant you had to go through a door before your dog, you had to eat before your dog ate, he wasn't allowed on the furniture but stayed on the floor, and you put him in his place over and over. WHAT THE ACTUAL HELL?

There were just one or two MASSIVE PROBLEMS with this! The theory was based on unrelated captive wolves who had been put in artificial packs in a zoo rather than wild wolves who lived in family units consisting of parents and their pups. And the study assumed that wolves and dogs were the *same*. But dogs and wolves are separated by TENS OF THOUSANDS of years of evolution and DNA. They are not the same creature AT ALL.

Mech ended up debunking his own theory and begging his publishers to stop printing his book, but the idea had taken hold and assumed a life of its own and many dog trainers *still* train using this COMPLETELY INCORRECT theory! It's crazy!

From all my training and research, I see that dogs like to be LED and guided in the same way that children look to their parents to show them the ropes. It's NOT about who's the Alpha or 'top dog' or pack leader and who's in charge but instead it is about MUTUAL RESPECT. I am *sick* of people treating dogs like they're subservient. It's disgusting.

### Your dog is a three-year-old toddler

Let's forget about wolves, pack theory and Alphas and think instead about children and family units. I want to change your mindset.

I don't believe that there's any such thing as an ADULT dog. Instead, I believe that all dogs have the mental age of a THREE-YEAR-OLD TODDLER. Read that again. However old they are, dogs NEVER mentally outgrow a three-year-old toddler. Even if a dog is seventeen years old, they still have the mental needs of a three-year-old.

I have three kids, three grandchildren and I fostered twelve children, so I know a thing or two about kids. Dogs like consistency and routine, just like toddlers. Random things that seem totally normal to adults – balloons, buses, people shouting – can seem completely alien to a toddler. It's the same with dogs. I remember once wondering why Scooby was being so quiet and weird after my birthday. Was he upset that I didn't give him any cake? It took me a few days to realize it was the helium balloon in the corner of the room. He'd just stare at the floor, really still. If you change something in your home environment, it can really distress them.

Like children, dogs live in the present. They don't really have a concept of yesterday and tomorrow and only have a 72-hour memory for their environment.

I think if people understood that dogs never really grow up, it would make dog training so much easier because your expectations would be so different. You would make allowances instead of getting mad that your dog was displaying puppyish tendencies.

Would you expect your toddler to be fully potty trained in a week? OF COURSE NOT. And yet we put all this pressure on dogs from a super young age and get mad when they have accidents in the house. It takes *months* for a toddler to learn how to use a potty and then a toilet but dogs are expected to get it straight away. Or we leave them alone in the house and they wreck something and we get mad at them.

Don't look at WHAT they've done but WHY they've done it. With dogs and puppies, there is ALWAYS a reason behind the behaviour. One hundred per cent of the time. Dogs don't do things just because they want to do it. They want to please you. Any issues like chewing, aggression or destructive habits, the whole book of behavioural issues, they ALL happen for a reason. They're not just born that way.

Switch your brain and the way you train and you'll get different results.

## Your role as paw-rent

When you think of your dog as a toddler, it helps you to understand your role – as the PARENT. This means that it is YOUR job to keep your dog safe and to set boundaries for him. A boundary is NOT the same as dominance or pack theory. And boundaries are set and followed with mutual respect, not bullying.

It's very important that you remember that you're the parent and they're the child and you need to take control of each situation. You have to be responsible. Just like you wouldn't let your toddler set their own bed time or eat whatever they liked – ice cream for breakfast anyone? – you shouldn't be letting your dog make those big decisions.

On top of keeping them safe, like a toddler, they'll want a random cuddle or a fuss for five minutes.

## Autism and dogs

In my thirties, I worked with children and young adults with autism and severe, challenging behaviour in a residential unit. I'm not trying to be controversial, but from my time working with young adults and children with autism, I saw a lot of similarities with how dogs respond anxiously to things like bright lights and loud noises and find new or unfamiliar environments and situations upsetting. I believe that most dogs are on the spectrum and tweaking our thinking in this respect could really help our relationship with our dogs.

Dogs' hearing is much more sensitive than ours and yet our homes are often filled with noise all day long – the radio and TV are on, the children are screaming, we're shouting from room to room. Sensory overload is really common in dogs. We have to consider how all these things make our dogs feel – they're part of the family too.

A classic thing that I see people do is leave the TV or radio on for their dogs when they're left alone in the house. You think the dog will feel less alone but you could be making it worse for a dog that is sensitive to noise. Or they might just really hate that radio station! You'd be better leaving it quiet with low lights, a nice calm environment.

## The power of dog

We don't give dogs the credit they deserve. Think of all the human diseases that dogs can detect, the power they have to completely change a person's life, to provide comfort, to guide someone who is blind. They're like a higher power. They communicate in ways that we don't even understand, yet we think *we're* the higher power. For a dog to be able to talk to another dog without verbal language, as I see daily in my day care, is fascinating.

The Ancient Egyptians had the dog god, Anubis, who was the 'guide of souls'. Dogs were given great respect and mummified when they died before being buried in family tombs. They understood that dogs had a special power. They saw Anubis as a cross-over with the spirits who could talk in two worlds. I have a tattoo of Anubis on my arm. I'm obsessed with Ancient Egypt! I believe that all animals have a spirit, a soul, feelings and emotions.

But that DOESN'T mean we should *humanize* them. We misread our dogs constantly, putting their behaviour through a human lens. People say, 'Oh he's not happy, his hackles have gone up' or 'He's scared, his tail is between his legs.'

When a dog wees and another dog wees on top of it, we as humans see that as dominance. Going over his patch. That isn't it at all. It's a CALLING CARD. A dog can tell from another dog's smell what the personality of the dog is. They wee on top because they're then leaving *their* calling card. It's a COMPLETE myth that it's about dominance. And when dogs do the little poo dance after they've pooped, they're trying to get the smell in the air for other dogs. Clever. But not nice when you're bent over picking up dog poo and your dog is flicking it all in your face! Thanks a lot!

Dogs have different taste buds to us. Owners often find it hard to understand that a dog's diet should stay the same because they put themselves in their place. 'What? They've got to eat chicken every day for the rest of their life? That's cruel. They'll get bored!' With dogs it's about the smell but also texture, which is why a good-quality raw diet works so well for them, as we explore in Chapter 3.

Another thing I hear constantly when a dog is barking at other dogs on the lead or being aggressive in the house is, 'He's protecting me.' Sorry to burst that bubble but NO, it doesn't mean he's protecting you. He's not showing his undying love for you. He's GUARDING you like a resource, like you're his food or a toy as we discover with Jasper the Jack Russell in the Aggression in the House case study in Chapter 9.

When you can see your dog *clearly*, you'll better understand his needs and how best to train him.

# Common myths about dogs

There are so many misconceptions about dogs that we all just automatically believe because they've been around for so long but I'm here to set the record straight:

- **Dogs only respect the Alpha in a group**
  This is proven to be untrue and is based on a now debunked theory. Dogs respond really well to leaders and a parent-child relationship, NOT being ruled by fear and dominance.

- **Dogs are protecting us when they bark at other dogs, people or moving things**
  If your dog seems to be protecting you from outside 'threats', don't be fooled into thinking it's because he loves you (sorry!). He's simply guarding his resource – YOU!

- **Dogs just know the basics**
  Without training, your dog does NOT know the difference between outside and inside for toilet training. He does NOT know the basic commands. He has to be trained.

- **Certain dog breeds are dangerous**
  All dogs are individuals. You can't group a whole breed as dangerous. I see this time and time again where other trainers have given up on a dog because he's a certain breed. I would never do that.

- **Dogs that hump are showing dominance**
  NOPE. If your dog is humping the table leg, his soft toys, or even you, it's not dominance. He's masturbating. It's perfectly natural. Male and female dogs do it.

# CHAPTER 3

# THE POWER OF THREE: DIET, ENVIRONMENT AND MENTAL STIMULATION

When I first start working with a dog, *whatever* their problem, I always look at THREE things:

1. DIET
2. ENVIRONMENT
3. MENTAL STIMULATION

No *one* thing is more or less important than the others; I look at them ALL because they tell me EVERYTHING about the dog. Throughout Part 2 of this book, you will see how I use these three things to assess each dog, and ultimately what combination of the three I use to fix them. Sometimes it will be one or two of these that need sorting, sometimes it's all three. But if your dog has an issue, always look at these three things and you'll find your answer.

## 1. Diet

Could your dog's diet be causing their behaviour or making it worse? Diet is a massive contributor to behaviour. As humans we're pretty knowledgeable about how food affects our mood. We talk about comfort eating and mood-boosting ingredients. We're more informed these days with the traffic light system on our food. We understand what too much salt, sugar and saturated fat can do to us. But we don't bring this same perspective to our dogs.

As a dog nutritionist I know the right balance a dog should have. And I've seen through my work with over 16,500 dogs that the wrong diet can contribute to everything from a dog's aggression to anxiety and depression. 'What do you feed your dog?' is always the first question I ask.

I usually ask an owner to guess how much meat is in their dog's diet and they are ALWAYS shocked. Some popular dog foods don't contain ANY meat. BIG FAT ZERO! And they're often the most expensive ones. It's absolutely shocking. You might be giving your dog an expensive food, thinking they're on a really healthy diet, but some of the most expensive dog foods are the worst. Expensive isn't always best. It's so important for dogs to have a complete balanced diet. Ideally a dog should have at least 70 per cent meat in their food.

There are a few things with diets that I see time and time again and I can spot them a MILE off.

### Cut the carbs

If I've got a dog with what I would call 'nervous energy' who is always on edge and a bit anxious, I would know before I've even looked at the diet that it's going to contain lots of carbs. Why? Because carbs turn to SUGAR. Like a kid ramped up on sweets, if your dog has an excess of carbs and sugar in their diet, they're going to be BOUNCING OFF THE WALLS.

Dog biscuits are often packed FULL of carbs – white potatoes, white rice, brown rice, sweet potatoes, corn, wheat, barley, oats – and some dogs are okay with that. But if your dog is anxious or nervous, look at cutting them out of his diet.

### Remove red meat

If your dog has aggression issues, either human aggression or dog-on-dog aggression, I would avoid a red meat diet containing beef, lamb, rabbit or duck. Red meat contributes massively to anger issues because it's full of testosterone. It's like injecting your dog with steroids. I saw a dog the other day who was a great example of too much testosterone through red meat. The dog had bitten someone last Christmas. As soon as I mentioned food and the importance of not giving a dog red meat, the owner said, 'Oh my God, we've been giving him more and more red meat for the last six months.' And it pinpointed the escalation of his behaviour. He hadn't been neutered. He already had testosterone coursing through his body and then they'd been *cramming* him full of red meat every day and it had created CHAOS. Instead of red meat, try chicken, turkey or fish.

### How to check your dog's diet

So now we know what to avoid, but what should we be looking for? It's easy to find out what's in your dog's food if you look in the right place. On the back of a packet of dog food, there will be a section called 'Composition'. It will list all the ingredients and the amount that's in your dog's food. Alternatively, most dog food companies have this information available on their websites.

Look out for meat content (which should be 70 per cent or higher) and what type of meat – red or white, animal derivatives (which is trash like ground chicken beaks and bits of hoof minced down –avoid avoid avoid) and carbs.

### Reach for raw: Why I recommend raw dog food

What's an ideal diet to feed your dog? I'm a vegan so the fact that I recommend a raw meat diet for dogs should show you HOW much I believe in it! A raw diet is the best thing for a dog, nutritionally and psychologically.

When people think of raw meat, they think of it being all sloppy, bloody and messy when it's defrosted. But the reality couldn't be FURTHER from the truth. A good-quality raw meat, when defrosted, should still stay solid so you can slice through it with a knife. Out of a 1kg (2lb 4oz) tub, you should expect nothing more than two dessertspoons of blood.

Like anything, there is GOOD raw dog food and POOR raw dog food. A good-quality 'complete' raw food to me would be at least 70 per cent human-grade meat, 10 per cent ground-down bone, 10 per cent vegetables and 10 per cent offal. The vegetables in it should be pulped so you can't see any bits of veg. Just meat won't give your dog the nutrients he needs. A good test is your dog's poop. When a dog is on a good-quality raw food, their poop is completely odourless.

It's probably easiest for most people to buy a complete raw food from a supplier. There is a wide selection for you to choose from, depending on your dog's needs. You can buy raw food online or from good pet shops. Even as a qualified nutritionist, I wouldn't try to make my own raw dog food. It's so difficult to get the correct amount of vitamins and minerals, and manage the right ratios.

Although I don't advocate feeding a high-energy dog carbs because it turns to sugar, complex carbohydrates like sweet potatoes and brown rice can be a good way of adding fibre to their diet and can also help older dogs increase their energy levels. Dogs don't need any grain in their diet from a nutritional point of view. It's an unnecessary filler.

## How to feed raw

Raw food needs to be kept in the freezer until the day before you intend to feed it, when you swap it out to the fridge. It needs to be eaten within four days. Adult dogs should have two meals per day, puppies should have three.

Once dogs have lost their puppy teeth, they can have their raw diet five days a week and two days a week they have raw chicken wings. If you feed them raw chicken wings from six months onwards, twice a week, they will never need dental work such as teeth or plaque removed. The wings MUST be raw NOT cooked. The bone in the wings cleans their teeth and it's impossible for dogs to choke on them. It gives them really good bone content to keep their poop solid. I'd suggest chicken wing days are Tuesdays and Thursdays so it's not consecutive days, and on those days, they eat nothing but chicken wings.

People are often worried about feeding their dog bones. And you do need to be careful. The only bones I would ever give to a dog are RAW chicken wings and RAW chicken carcass. These are safe for dogs. Bones only splinter when they are cooked, which is why we always feed them raw. Dogs shouldn't eat butcher's bones. They're often from red meat animals and can chip a dog's teeth or make them weak. In complete dog food, the bone is ground down so you don't have to worry about it.

### Alternatives to raw food

If you don't want to feed your dog raw food, the next best thing is cold-pressed food. It's a dry dog food that comes in pellets so it's easy to feed – direct from bag to bowl. Cold-pressed dog food is gently pressed with much less heat and processing than traditional kibble, meaning the essential nutrients and minerals remain. The pellets break down gently and prevent bloating. In comparison, kibble is cooked at high temperatures and pressed tightly using a process called 'extrusion'. This means that nutrients can get lost and makes the food harder for your dog to digest.

### Tackle the treats

Once you've sorted out your dog's diet, don't forget to look at the treats you give him. Everyone is obsessed with treat and food training. I point out to people that they've given their dog a treat just for sitting in front of them and I say, 'Oh do you do that with your child?' Of course they don't. Here's a bag of sweets, well done for blinking. Here's another packet of sweets, well done for watching the TV, here's another, well done for having a little drink. Ridiculous. But that's what we do constantly with our dogs.

A good test is every time you want to give your dog a treat – for eating his breakfast, for coming back off your walk, for sitting down, before bed – put it in a jar instead. Owners are ALWAYS surprised when I ask them to do this because at the end of the day, the jar is almost full. There's no harm giving your dog an *occasional* treat but stuffing them full of them morning, noon and night isn't what we should be doing! It's like us having the biscuit barrel next to the kettle. Before you know it, you're three packets of biscuits deep. If you're constantly giving your dog a treat, try moving the treat jar out of sight.

Treats like gravy bones and dental sticks are full of carbs and sugar. It's like washing your dog's teeth with a burger. You might be giving them a healthier diet and then ruining it with treats. If you want to give your dog a little treat, go for chicken, frankfurter or cheese. A small cube is plenty. You don't need to be chucking packs of sausages at him or a wheel of cheese!

## Serve supplements

If you get a good 'complete' dog food it should include everything – fish oil, vitamins and minerals. For a large-breed dog I would also add green-lipped mussel – this powder is ten times more potent than glucosamine and it's a natural anti-inflammatory so it's fantastic for their joints and gut health. I take it daily too!

If you can't afford, or don't want, to feed raw – but still want your dog to get all the essential nutrients and minerals he needs – try my Nutri-bomb. I created the recipe for people who want to give their dogs the best but might struggle to do that. A sprinkle of this magic powder topper on your dog's food every day will give him everything he needs – vital vitamins, minerals, antioxidants and brain food – to keep him in great health and condition. All the ingredients are natural. It contains coconut flakes, turmeric, sage, thyme, ground celery seeds, parsley, wild nettle, curly kale, parsnips, broccoli, carrots, sea kelp and psyllium husk. This combination can:

- Help keep fleas at bay and prevent ear yeast infections
- Decrease inflammation and alleviate arthritic pain
- Support a healthy nervous system
- Eliminate toxins
- Aid the digestive system and gut health
- Alleviate dry, itchy skin and promote a glossy coat
- Improve cognitive behaviour
- Boost the immune system

## Make meal times work

A fully grown dog should eat two meals per day, ideally around 7–8am, after their morning walk, and between 4 and 5pm, no later. Dogs should ALWAYS be fed AFTER exercise not before in any circumstance. Dogs can get bloat or a twisted stomach from exercising too soon after a meal. You wouldn't go to the gym when you'd just eaten. Being consistent with what your dog eats and when he eats gives him the security and routine that he needs. Having grown up in a household where one day you'd get dinner and the next you wouldn't, I understand the importance of consistency.

I don't believe there's any such thing as a fussy eater and I have a host of tips to sort out this issue. Check out my case study with Bella the Welsh Terrier in Chapter 15. Dogs are driven by food so getting their food when they get home from a walk is like a treat. You give them their food, they've had their physical exercise, had some mental stimulation, and then they'll have a good sleep.

### Changing your dog's diet

If you decide to change your dog's food to raw, you need to do this carefully so you don't upset their digestive system. Normally, swapping from one type of kibble to another, you would change it slowly over the course of a week. Start by adding a small amount of the new food to your dog's original food – around 25 per cent – and then gradually increase it until by the end of the week, your dog is completely on the new food. But with raw food, you can't feed a dog a mixture of raw and kibble because they digest at different rates, making it dangerous to combine. You have to do the swap in one go. Never start giving your dog raw food on a day they've had kibble, instead start on a 'clean' day. Crack two raw eggs with the shell over their first raw meal. The eggshell cleans out their system. When clients swap their dogs onto raw food, I get them to send me photos of their dog's poop. GROSS! But I can tell from looking at it if there's too much or not enough bone content, for example. The poop should be solid, squeezing it out like bullets. One of the benefits is that it stops dogs suffering with anal gland issues because it squeezes them as it empties out.

Start on fish or white meat as a gentle way in and make sure when you serve it, for the first time especially, that you serve it at room temperature and not straight from the fridge, which could cause a chill on the dog's stomach. They might vomit it back up if not. Always make sure you're feeding the right amount for your dog as well – check the manufacturer's guidelines.

### 2. Environment

It's really important that you have a good, hard look at your home environment – both as a whole house and within each individual room. We get blind to our own homes, familiarity making it hard to see clearly. Try to look at it from the point of view of a stranger – or me – and assess each zone of the house. Ask yourself, 'Does the dog have access here? Should he? Are there dangers or hazards? Is it a chaotic mad house with children screaming and mess everywhere? Has anything changed recently?' Be honest and then you'll start to see where your dog's issues are coming from.

As soon as I walk into a house on my private home visits, my eyes are EVERYWHERE. The second I'm through the front door I'm making mental notes, not on the colour of the walls (Magnolia? Really?) or the style of soft furnishings (Where did you get that throw from?) but on whether there's a safety gate to keep an aggressive dog away from the front door, where the dog's bed is located, how noisy the house is, how tidy the rooms are, who lives there, are there children or other pets? These are all things that might be contributing to a dog's bad behaviour.

Like a toddler, as discussed in Chapter 2, your dog needs the security of feeling safe within his environment. He needs routine, consistency and boundaries. He needs to know where he can and can't go, and he needs to have a place he can escape to when things get too much – the equivalent of a child's bedroom. You HAVE to have a routine for your dog. He should know what time to get up and go to sleep, what time he's walked and fed. It doesn't have to be to the exact millisecond, we're not the army, but it needs to be within the same parameters each day.

## Your dog's bed

Your dog's bed should be their SAFE HAVEN away from everything else, tucked in a corner, furthest away from everything. Dogs have a strong fight or flight response. Having an ESCAPE PLAN – somewhere to run off to – means they're much less likely to 'fight' if they feel uncomfortable. A dog's bed should never be in a hallway because there's too much traffic with people coming and going. This is especially important for a dog with aggression or guarding issues. The hallway usually leads to the front door, which for dogs who go mad when visitors come to the house or when post gets mailed, is another no-no.

I recommend crates because they give the vibe of a cosy den. You can cover them over with blankets or towels to make them snug, and keep the door open so they can come and go as they please. I know a lot of people have issues with dog crates and see them as punishment but crates are only punishment if you USE them as punishment. I talk more about crate training in Chapter 5. If you have a destructive dog, it's important to carefully choose their bedding and make sure there's nothing they can ingest. If that's the case, play it safe with a hard-wearing plastic bed with vet bedding. It's the safest option and non-toxic.

When I ask people where their dog sleeps, most people pull a face and say, super apologetically, 'In the bedroom.' I'm ALL for your dog sleeping in your bedroom. I loved cosy cuddle time with Scooby on the bed. I don't have an issue with it where most behaviourists would! I want to let people know that it's fine. It's not weird behaviour. It's not a big NO-NO. I only have an issue with it if your dog is growling when you get into bed or turn over in the night. They're guarding the bed in that case, as we cover in Chapter 11.

### Access all areas

Dogs often have unlimited access to the whole house. I'm *always* surprised by the number of homes I visit with problem dogs who are just allowed to roam free. Safety gates are your training best friend. If you have an aggressive dog or an escape-artist, you should be restricting their access to the hallway and front door. But we don't just want to shut that dog away and close the door. Most aggression stems from FEAR. Think of a three-year-old toddler who is scared. You close the door but behind it they can hear noises. They're going to be even more terrified because they'll imagine this big scary monster. You're making the situation worse. Instead, use a safety gate. A gate is a barrier but they can still see and hear through it, which, I've witnessed in other cases, takes their anxiety levels down by up to 60 per cent.

### Red zones

I've mentioned the hallway and front door, but that's just one RED ZONE in your home. A red zone is a NO-GO DOG ZONE. This is a part of the house where your dog doesn't NEED to be and, for his and everyone's safety, he SHOULDN'T be. Depending on your dog's issue, other red zones could include the kitchen, the playroom, the dining room and the bedrooms. These should be zoned off so your dog can't access them. You wouldn't have a toddler running around the kitchen while you're cooking so why do you have your bouncy puppy in there? Dogs in the kitchen are dangerous – they can jump up, knock pans over, get food that they shouldn't have and trip you up. WHOOPS.

Yet dogs' beds are often in the kitchen and even if they're not, most dogs have full access all the time because the door to the garden is often situated there. If that's the case, think about where else in the house you could put your dog's bed and when it's time to go to the toilet, you can simply guide your dog through the kitchen to the garden and then bring him straight back out. If you have a dog that's a menace near food, then keeping him out of the kitchen will do wonders for your sanity and shopping bills!

If you have small children, you might not want the dog in their bedrooms or playroom. Safety gates keep everyone safe. The clue is in the name!

We encourage dogs to play in the living room, then when we're watching our favourite TV show, we say, 'Oh God STOP squeaking that ball!' as they repeatedly drop it at our feet. That annoying habit has been caused by YOU because you've taught the dog that that room is a playroom. How does your dog understand that certain rooms have certain limits? If he's not used to playing with his toys in the living room then he won't see that room as a play room.

### Toys and noise

Are your dog's toys lying around everywhere? Are there children in the house? Are the dogs and children's toys mixed together? These are RED FLAGS I would look for. Your dog's toys shouldn't be littered all over the floor (we discuss this further in the Mental Stimulation section) and it is not a good thing to have the dog's and kids' toys mixed together. It's something we accept – 'We have a dog, we have a thousand dog toys' – and you see something when you are out with the kids and you say, 'He'd love that, look at the little squeaky thing.' And now you live in the toy aisle of a pet shop. Your dog needs to know WHICH are his toys and WHEN he can play with them.

Dogs can easily get overstimulated or anxious from too much noise. You might have a noisy house with the TV on all the time, the radio, the vacuum going, children shouting and singing. And that's fine IF your dog is okay with it or he has somewhere to escape. I've seen it multiple times. The children are screaming and carrying on, and you've got a dog that's very playful and pulling at the kids' clothes and they think it's a game and so does the dog.

And then he nips them. You can't really blame the dog for that. It's like a red rag to a bull. You have to be sensitive to his needs and either TURN THE DIAL DOWN a few notches or give him his own calm space.

Arguments can also really upset your dog. They're sensitive creatures and understand a lot more than we give them credit for. Just like children, they pick up on tension and fighting so try to restrict this kind of interaction. I know it's not easy if you're going through a separation or divorce but you really do have to think about your pets too. We look at this in more detail in the separation anxiety case study with Bobby the Labrador in Chapter 14.

Maybe you have other pets – other dogs, cats, rabbits – that are adding to your dog's poor behaviour. If you're going to be bringing a new pet into the family, make sure you introduce them to your dog properly. Not with formal handshakes and welcome drinks but by making sure it's a safe, calm environment, allowing them to get used to each other. Every pet is different so make sure you do this carefully. If you have a rescue animal, make sure you follow any advice from the rescue centre.

## How to introduce new pets to your dog

1. If you're introducing a new dog or puppy to your dog, make sure they meet first on neutral ground. Keep both dogs on the lead to start with.
2. Arrange three or four meet-ups on neutral ground before letting the dogs meet in the house.
3. The new dog has to learn mutual respect. So many people introduce a new puppy to an older dog and then blame the older dog when he gets frustrated with the new puppy. That's not fair.
4. If you're introducing a cat to your dog, put your dog on a lead. Let the cat explore the new surroundings. Do this for 10–15 minutes each day until they're desensitized to each other. When the cat turns his back on the dog, you'll know he's comfortable.
5. Whatever pet you're bringing in to the house, always do it in a calm, safe, controlled environment.

### Do you need another dog?

If your dog is misbehaving or chewing things out of boredom, do NOT get another dog to 'keep him company'. It NEVER works. Getting another dog will NOT solve your dog's behavioural issues and you'll have TWO dogs with problems. People also think that if they have two dogs then they don't need to send them to day care while they're at work because they'll occupy each other – 'She'll keep him company.' Instead, you'll have two dogs in the house alone for two four-hour blocks of time with maybe an hour in the middle when a dog walker lets them out. NO. JUST NO. We look at destructive siblings in Chapter 18 and the problems that can come from having multiple dogs in the house.

## 3. Mental stimulation

Mental stimulation is like exercise for your dog's brain. Dogs don't just need physical exercise; they need MENTAL EXERCISE too. It involves activities and challenges that make them think, learn and solve problems. A bit like us doing a sudoku! Just as regular dog walks keep your dog fit and healthy (and are a part of mental stimulation too), it's important to keep their minds occupied – vital for dogs with challenging behaviour. An added bonus is that it often tires them out too.

### Wonderful walkies

Your dog should be getting two walks a day. Depending on his size and age, those walks might vary in distance and type. You might have an older dog with arthritis who is happy to potter around the park saying hello to old friends, or you might have a hyper dog that's happy to run for miles. Daily walks aren't just about exercise, they are a chance to bond with your dog, and for him to have some freedom and socialize with his peers. It's VITAL to your dog's mental health that he's stimulated in this way.

Make sure you mix it up every so often – take a trip to the coast and walk him along the beach, letting him paddle in the sea, or take him on a hike with some doggy pals to a new place full of new smells and sensations.

If you're struggling to walk your dog either because of time or health issues, first of all stop feeling guilty. I've spoken to *so* many owners who are making themselves sick with guilt. And secondly get some help – that might be a local dog walker, that might mean sending your dog to doggy day care twice a week, or it might mean asking family members. If your dog has poor recall, you could hire a dog field to let him have a run around safely without the fear that he'll run off.

We cover *everything* from poor recall to pulling on the lead in the case studies in Part 2, so if your walkies are anything *but* wonderful, head there for some tips and training plans.

### Toy time

This is one that everyone can do, starting right now. We've already talked about how I don't like to see dog toys scattered all over the house, but here's another reason why. I could record your dog for 24 hours and in that time, there would probably be about 7 minutes where he plays with or interacts with his toys. He gets bored of them if they're hanging around all the time, like a dull person at a party.

Instead of having them on the floor ALL the time, keep the dog toys in a basket, out of sight. Then twice a day, mid-morning and mid-afternoon, bring the basket out, tip it onto the floor and let him choose his toys and have structured PLAY TIME. Let him go crazy, interact with him, let him play how he wants to. He gets your full attention for 30–45 minutes. That structured play time gives him more mental stimulation in those two 45-minute slots than 24 hours with full access to his toys. It's also a great way to make sure a destructive dog still has play time. Because you're monitoring his toy use, he won't be able to tear limbs off his teddies or shred his ball. It also stops your dog repeatedly bringing you toys to throw when you're trying to watch your latest crime drama on Netflix later in the day.

### Puzzle problems

You can buy mental stimulation games but they are expensive and they last most dogs about two minutes because they're so intelligent. Then once they've solved it, you might as well chuck it away because he can do it and it's no longer mentally stimulating. There are much easier and cheaper ways to make sure your dog is getting his mental stimulation quota so save your cash and read on.

## Play dates and doggy day care

Just like you might meet friends for a coffee or catch up with other parents in the playground, you can organize play dates for your dog. They get to visit their friend and enjoy a little social time. And it doesn't cost you anything. Try for twice a week for no longer than an hour. Even if you live somewhere really rural and don't know many people, you can get on Facebook or a local community board and see if anyone fancies meeting up. Make sure you're safe about it – we don't want people going off meeting strangers in deserted places!

In an ideal world, your dog would go to doggy day care a couple of times a week. The mental stimulation dogs get from mixing with their peers and socializing in these environments sorts them out for the WHOLE week. At The Lodge, we provide a safe, supervised, fun environment set in three acres of woodland. Day care is great for socialization, for peer-to-peer learning, and will tire your dog out so he's not coming home and destroying his environment or driving you mad tap-dancing on tables for attention.

## Hydrotherapy hour

Hydro isn't just for injured animals; you can book a weekly or monthly session for a FUN activity. Find your local registered hydrotherapy pool and ask if they do fitness swims where your dog can go and play with a ball for an hour in the water. The hydrotherapist will be in the water with them or some places encourage you to get in too. They have a life jacket on, and the water is nice and warm. It's complete mental stimulation because the dog has to think about all four legs moving in a certain direction. It fries their brain, in a good way, and gives them a massive endorphin boost.

## Agility and flyball activities

If you can afford it, agility and flyball – where dogs do obstacle courses against the clock or relay races over hurdles using a spring-loaded tennis ball – are GREAT fast-paced fun. Your dog must be at least 18 months old for these kinds of activities. But they can be expensive or the travel might prevent you getting to them. If that's the case, fear not – set up a little obstacle course in your garden or even inside your house. Just make sure you move the vase your aunt Jackie bought you for your wedding! You can use canes or sticks in the ground or those little cones. It doesn't need to be expensive. Have FUN with it. Don't just set up the course for them to play alone but use it as an activity that you do WITH them – half an hour's agility every Thursday morning.

Not a fan of agility? Try hide and seek. Hide one of their toys, rather than food, and get them to search high and low for it. People play games like this with their children but don't think to do it with their dog. Think how much your toddler or grandchildren love it; your dog would too.

# CHAPTER 4

# BASIC TRAINING PRINCIPLES

Before we get into the nitty-gritty, I want to take a look at some of the BASICS of what I'm teaching. Like building a house, you have to get your foundation right before you can add a single brick. Training is the same.

### Leon's ten canine commandments

When you're training your dog, keep these ten basic rules in mind at all times and you won't go wrong.

## 1. Reward good behaviour and ignore unwanted behaviour

Positive reinforcement is the only way of training I endorse. I use kind, loving techniques because they work, time after time, as I've seen with the thousands of dogs I've treated. Just like children, shouting and screaming will make matters worse. It is not going to help them get over the problem they've got. It's just going to scare them, making them feel intimidated and vulnerable.

## 2. Be consistent

Your dog has to understand the dos and don'ts of his environment. He will only do that if you – and everyone who interacts with him – are consistent. That means using the same commands and rewards, and praising or ignoring the same behaviours. If you have a dog that jumps up and you say DOWN and your partner says OFF, your dog will be confused and won't understand.

Agree as a household what commands you'll use. You could write them down and stick them on the fridge.

### 3. Communicate clearly

Make sure YOU know what you want your dog to do, then communicate it really clearly. Ask yourself, 'What am I asking the dog to do and does he understand?' Dogs only understand one-word commands. Don't bury your command in the middle of a long sentence, or make it sound like a question. Say the word ONCE and say it clearly. Give your dog a chance to respond before you repeat it. Make sure your tone matches your command. Are you saying COME in a bored, flat voice or are you making your recall sound exciting and fun?

### 4. Be patient

Your dog wants to do the right thing. Trust me. No dog wants to disappoint their owner so give him time to get it right. Shouting a command twenty times one after the other won't work and getting frustrated with your dog because he hasn't got the hang of training *immediately* is unfair. Manage your expectations. Remember he's the equivalent of a three-year-old child.

### 5. Take timing seriously

When you're training your dog, you need to reward at the right moment, not five minutes later or when you get home. You need to make a BIG song and dance at the moment they do something great. Get your cheerleading pom-poms out and do those high-kicks! If you get your timing wrong, your dog won't understand what he's been praised for or will mistake the behaviour he thinks you want him to repeat.

### 6. Progress at your dog's pace

Remember that *every* dog is different so go at YOUR dog's pace, not at the pace your friend's dog went at or what you think would be good progress. There will be days when you take one step forward and five back. Suck it up and move on. Gradual progress that your dog understands will become learned behaviour that lasts a lifetime rather than a flash-in-the-pan trick you teach. Do it step by step, take your time, and don't rush it.

## 7. Socialize your way to success

So many of the problems I see on a daily basis could have been entirely prevented through solid socialization as a puppy. Socializing your puppy between the ages of three and twelve weeks is key. You can't normally collect your puppy until he's eight weeks old, giving you four short weeks to positively introduce your pup to as many different things as you can – traffic, children, other animals, different environments, a range of sounds. Before your dog is fully vaccinated, this will have to be done in your arms but once he's had his jabs, he can experience everything from the ground. WAHEY! HE'S OFF! Experiences in this period will influence how your dog feels about different or new situations as he grows older. A puppy who isn't well socialized will likely grow up into a nervous, scared dog. No one wants that!

## 8. Manage his motivation

If you want your dog to really *listen*, you need to think about what most motivates him and plan your training accordingly. Is it food, is it a ball or toy, or is it praise? WHO'S A GOOD BOY THEN? If food is your dog's main motivation, be careful you don't give him too many treats. I usually give dogs 5–10 treats MAX per training session while they're learning. Any more and they're just doing whatever you're asking for the food and then if there's a day you don't have a treat, you're in deep trouble.

## 9. Practise regularly

You want to make sure that you practise your new training techniques enough times that your dog gets what you want him to do, but not so many times that it's overkill. Once your dog's attention span has moved on to something more interesting, note your progress for the day or week and move on. You don't want him to be bored!

## 10. End on a positive note

Whether your session has gone well or you want to go and SCREAM into a cupboard, always end on a positive note so that your dog doesn't get stressed out by his training and will be willing to try again next time you give it a go.

Now you've got the basics nailed, let's get into COMMANDS.

## Doggy sign language

On the front inside cover of this book you'll find a QR code. Hover your phone over it and it will take you through to my exclusive training videos so you can watch me as I train a dog in my eight basic commands. You'll see how I use my doggy sign language to get the dog to do what I want him to do and you'll be able to do the same with your dog. EASY!

When I teach a dog a specific word command like SIT or STAY, I match a hand movement with it. This way the dog learns to associate the word and movement together so that after a while, I can take away the verbal command and just use the sign language. It's really handy if you're in the park and you need them to STAY or tell them NO but they're far away. You can do the hand sign without them needing to hear you.

When I talk about high-value treats in this section, I'm talking cheese, frankfurter, chicken. It needs to be something your dog isn't getting every day, that SMELLS good. It only needs to be small amounts; you don't need to cart an entire hot dog stand to the field with you! It's the quality not the quantity in this case.

With all these commands, don't try to teach them all in one day. It will only confuse your dog. Take your time and make sure he's mastered one before starting the next. There will be a natural progression through them.

The eight main commands I teach dogs are:

| | |
|---|---|
| SIT | LEAVE |
| STAY | GO |
| UP | NO |
| OFF | |
| COME | |

### Teaching your dog to SIT

Teaching your dog to SIT is a relatively easy one to start with because it's a natural movement for dogs. Get your dog to stand in front of you and purse your fingers together in a 'chef's kiss' style as though you're holding something in your fingers (either hand will do). Raise your hand up and say SIT. If done properly his head will follow your hand moving upwards and naturally his bottom will touch the floor as he goes backwards. It's a bit of a trick really. Praise him and reward him with a treat. Repeat. Once your dog has learned the command, stop with the treats. Be aware that some dogs like Dachshunds, can't sit properly so don't teach them to sit.

### Teaching your dog to STAY

This command is easier if your dog is sitting down. So, get him into the SIT position first. The hand action for STAY is a raised flat hand. Hold your flat hand out in front of you. Have a treat in your other hand. Get your dog to focus on the treat. Bring the treat towards your flat raised hand and say STAY – STAY. Then GO (see below) is the release.

### Teaching your dog UP

To teach UP, I pat my chest with both hands and say UP in an encouraging tone. Once he's jumped up, give him a treat. Repeat this 5–10 times. Once he's got the hang of it, no more treats.

### Teaching OFF

Your dog can only learn OFF, once he knows UP. As soon as he has learned the command UP, get him to jump UP and instead of giving him a treat, point to the side and say OFF. As you say OFF and point, take half a step back so that he'll naturally come to the floor without any physical interaction. Then give him a treat. Repeat. This is a great command for getting your dog off sofas and beds.

### Teaching your dog to COME

We talk about this in depth in our recall case study in Chapter 7 but you're going to want a squeaky toy and a matching high-pitched voice. There's no hand command, it looks more like you pretending to be a jack-in-the-box, leaping up and down. You're going to dial your energy levels up to A MILLION and you are going to do *everything* in your power to make yourself look and sound as exciting and fun as possible for your dog. You're going to call your dog's name to get his attention and then GO FOR IT. Shout COME and jump up and down as though you're going for gold on the trampoline! Squeak the toy at the same time. When he comes to you, reward him with a high-value treat and lots of praise.

### Teaching your dog to LEAVE

LEAVE and WAIT are the same command, it's up to you on your word choice. If you prefer WAIT just swap that word for LEAVE. The hand sign for LEAVE is to make an 'L' of your thumb and first finger, like the sign for 'Loser'. Put it in front of your face and then move it out away from you with an outstretched arm. Have a treat in your other hand and get the dog to focus on the treat. Bring the treat towards the 'L' hand and then outstretch your 'L' hand saying LEAVE – LEAVE. He will associate the hand movement with the treat. Then put the treat on the floor but keep eye-contact the whole time. He will naturally take his eyes off the treat and look at the 'L'. Say LEAVE in a firm but fair tone. Leave a large pause and then repeat it once to keep him focused on your hand.

### Teaching GO

The signal for GO is the thumb and forefinger of the LEAVE 'L' held on its side to point like an arrow. Say GO in an energetic voice and give the treat. Repeat. Once they've got it, no more treats.

### Teaching NO

This is an important one for delinquents. To teach NO, turn your 'L' towards them, pointing at them, and say NO in a firm voice. Nine times out of ten, they'll look at you and start doing what they were going to do very slowly. Pause. Then say NO again with eye contact. Reward and repeat.

## Treat-based training

Traditional trainers and books are obsessed with treat-based training. But it doesn't work. And here's why. If you always use food, your dog is only doing the command for the food. If you're giving your dog a treat for every UP, he'll jump up on stuff on purpose, waiting for his treat. And if you give him a treat for OFF, he'll still jump up in order to jump off and get the treat. This is how we end up being TREAT-DRIVEN. It's caused by over-rewarding.

If you take the food away or you run out of treats one day and you haven't got the goods, he's not going to listen. Instead, use treats 5–10 times for him to understand the concept of whatever the command is and then once he understands the command, motivate him by giving him plenty of praise instead.

## NILFF – Nothing in Life for Free

It's important when you're training your dog to reward GOOD behaviour and ignore unwanted behaviour. It's really important when you're giving your dog a treat as a reward that he gets NILFF – Nothing in Life for Free. You should only reward the desired behaviour, not partial behaviour. If you ask your dog to SIT and he slightly lowers his back end before getting back up, he DOES NOT get a treat. If you ask him to COME and he gallops past you and carries on messing around, don't reward him. He only gets the treat for the behaviour you WANT, not a half attempt at it.

## The Drip-feed Technique

If your dog is anxious about certain social situations like going to the vet or being around other dogs, try my unique Drip-feed Technique. We cover this in more detail in the fear aggression case study in Chapter 19. When a dog is stressed, licking helps relax and soothe him. We can use this natural behaviour to help your dog with his anxiety. Using a block of Brussels pâté, ideally frozen so he can't scoff the lot in one go, we encourage him to LICK – not eat – the pâté to help turn his NEGATIVE trigger – the vet, loud noises, other dogs – into a POSITIVE experience. This will take time and repetition. As always, start small and build up in time. Once he's fixed, stop using the pâté.

## Avoidance techniques

Unlike other dog trainers, I don't believe in avoidance techniques because they don't FIX the problem, they simply DIVERT your dog's attention. This might look like throwing food on the floor to DISTRACT your dog from something he's scared of, also called 'scatter feeding', or it might look like a physical BLOCKING of your dog's vision if he sees another dog, or a bin truck or something that frightens him.

Diversion and avoidance can also PROLONG or cause unwanted behaviour. What do you think happens if your puppy is chewing the table leg and you DIVERT him with a chew? He thinks, 'She must really like that I'm chewing the table leg because she's given me a reward for it. I'll eat this chew first and then I'll carry on with the table leg because she'll probably give me another treat.'

Instead of avoidance, we should be looking to FIX the dog.

# CHAPTER 5

# BEING A RESPONSIBLE OWNER

There's a lot more to owning a dog than just finding one you like and bringing it home to the family. You owe it to your dog to treat him safely and responsibly. This chapter looks at all the ways you can do that.

## Walking on a lead

There are certain places your dog should ALWAYS be on a lead – by the side of a busy road, in a public park, or crowded areas. Being able to walk your dog safely on a lead is an important skill to learn. If you use an extendable lead, do me a favour and get rid of it, right now! I HATE THE THINGS!

We cover issues like recall and pulling on the lead, as well as aggression on the lead, in Part 2. But for now, my basics for walking on the lead are:

- When your dog is a puppy, get him used to the lead from the start. Every time he goes to the toilet in the garden, pop his lead on. Do ten minutes every day. That way it won't become a big thing when he's finally able to go outside properly after his jabs.
- Practise walking your dog around your garden, or a safe place, make sure you do plenty of start and stop practice.
- If your dog is pulling on the lead, stop and change direction. Every time he pulls, change direction. Don't be tempted to yank on the lead.

- Hold the lead in ONE hand, not two. This goes against a lot of common guidance but I've seen so many people fall and break wrists and ribs from holding it in two hands.
- Don't wrap the lead round and round your hand. If your dog pulls, he's going to break your fingers.
- Hold the lead in the hand furthest from the road (if you're walking along a road). A lot of guidance tells you to only hold the lead in your left hand. But what if that's right next to a busy road and your dog lunges into traffic? Always keep yourself between your dog and any traffic like you would with a toddler.
- Don't let him wander along the grass verge next to a road on a long lead. He could easily injure himself if he gets too close to the traffic.
- Your dog should walk NEXT to you, not behind or in front. His nose should be level with your front foot as you walk and your arm should be relaxed down by your side, not stretched out in front.

## Crate training

People can be quite scared of crates. Maybe it's the name – they don't sound exactly COSY, do they? Or maybe it's the metal bars giving prison vibes? But if you start to see them as DOGGY DENS, you see them in a whole new light. Dogs need somewhere safe and snug to call their own. But how do you introduce your dog to his new crate?

First of all, make sure your crate is the right size. Most people go too big. Your dog should be able to lie down full-length, stretched out, stand up and do a full 360-degree circle. But he doesn't need something the size of a ballroom!

Make the crate as appealing as possible. Cover it with blankets or towels to create a dark, tranquil space. Put their bedding and some toys inside. To get your dog used to it, feed him in there with the door open. Simply put his food bowl in and then ignore him – watching out of the corner of your eye – so it doesn't seem like a big deal. Your dog will quickly learn this is a positive place to be – COMFORT! FOOD! – and that he can come and go as he likes.

Never send your dog to their crate or lock them in as punishment. It's cruel and they'll develop a fear of it.

## Microchipping

Microchipping your dog is a legal requirement in many countries. It can be done easily and painlessly (for your dog if not your pocket) at your regular vet centre. A small microchip with a unique code is put under your dog's skin, usually on the neck, and this can be scanned to check his identity. Thousands of pets are lost and stolen each year and this gives you the BEST chance of being reunited if that happens. A collar and tag (also a UK legal requirement in public) can be removed but a microchip cannot. Keep a record of your dog's unique number and keep the database up-to-date with your contact details – address and phone number – so if he's ever lost or stolen, you can be contacted – and reunited – easily.

## Vaccinations

Vaccinations keep your dog healthy by protecting him from canine distemper, parvovirus, leptospirosis and parainfluenza and they prevent disease spreading among other dogs. Kennel cough is a separate treatment, given annually, via a nasal spray. There are multiple strains of kennel cough and the vaccine only covers one of those. Kennel cough has a ten-day incubation period and it's airborne, so your dog could catch it walking past a lamp post. They don't have to come into contact with another dog.

Puppies are usually vaccinated at 8–10 weeks old, with a second dose 2–4 weeks later. They will then need a booster at six or twelve months. If you're getting a rescue dog from a rehoming centre, you will get his vaccination card detailing what he's had and when. You should also regularly worm and deflea your dog. I also support holistic treatments for worming and flea treatments – one of the reasons I created the Nutri-bomb (see Chapter 3).

## Regular vet check ups

As soon as you get your puppy or rescue dog, you should get him checked out by the vet. Throughout his life, you should be making regular visits to check his health. If your dog has suddenly started displaying any behavioural concerns, your first step should always be a trip to the vet to rule out any health issues. Dogs constantly licking could have a yeast infection, dogs that are scared of loud noises might be reacting badly because of an ear infection, and dogs that are aggressive out of character might be in pain and keeping you away. Once health problems have been ruled out, you can carry on with your training plan.

---

### Pick up after your dog

Let's be blunt. NO ONE *likes* picking up dog poo. But it's your dog, your problem. I'm going to get bossy now because this is a pet peeve! Bag it up and pop it in the nearest bin or take it home with you. Don't bag it up and leave it hanging on a branch. It's not a poo tree! Don't leave a pile of it in the middle of the pavement for someone to stand in. And don't leave it on playing fields and parks where small children can get it in their eyes, causing toxocariasis which can lead to blindness. Be responsible.

---

### Notes on neutering

I'm pro-neutering but it has to be at the RIGHT time for the dog. Unless you're breeding from your dog, you should get them neutered. Spayed and neutered dogs live longer, healthier lives. It can reduce the risk of certain cancers – prostate in males, and ovarian, uterine and breast in females – and you don't have the worry of unwanted litters.

But a lot of people are given the WRONG advice and told to neuter their dog to solve all kinds of issues from aggression to humping. It's not *always* the right solution. And it's usually done FAR TOO SOON. I've seen dogs neutered at six months! WAAAAAAYYYYY too young. Doing it too early causes more problems than it solves.

Some doggy day care centres insist on only taking neutered dogs. Find another place if this is the case.

ALL dogs should be allowed to reach maturity before they are neutered or spayed. This is around 18 months in most breeds. Large breeds in particular need to be *at least* three years old before they're neutered so that they have enough testosterone or oestrogen to grow and develop as they should.

Neutering too soon can do the opposite of what you're trying to achieve. It can increase an aggressive dog's aggression – the very thing it's meant to help! It can create an absolute MONSTER. The only confidence a dog has comes from their testosterone (male) and oestrogen (female) and if you take that away and they're already of a nervous disposition, you're taking away any confidence they had in the first place. And they were already showing lack of confidence by being aggressive.

If you're unsure if neutering will help solve your dog's problem, try chemical castration. It lasts for six months, giving you time to try it out before you do the full job. You can get this for male and female dogs. If it makes the behaviour worse, or has no effect, at least it can be reversed.

## Muzzle training

When you read the word 'muzzle' you probably gave a little shudder. Be honest. They have a really bad reputation. I get it, they make your dog look like Hannibal Lector and we've been conditioned to give dogs like that a WIDE berth. But muzzles can be a really useful part of a rehabilitation programme. I NEVER use them as a permanent solution or punishment.

Dogs that require muzzle training tend to be human aggressive and dog-on-dog aggressive.

By using my FOUR-STEP MUZZLE METHOD you'll get great results with these unwanted behaviours.

Pick a muzzle that has a gap at the bottom so your dog can eat and drink but they can't bite. This introduction method also works for Haltis (which serve a different purpose and shouldn't be used instead of a muzzle). Follow the same advice but with your Halti.

1. Buy your muzzle but keep it in the box. Fill the box with frankfurters, Cheddar cheese or something high value with a really strong smell. Your dog will see the box and the muzzle for the very first time as a positive experience. So many people get a muzzle, take it out of the box, shove it on their dog's face and then wonder why they're freaking out. I'm not

surprised they don't like it! If you mess that first introduction up, you will have to buy another muzzle in a different colour.

2. Introduce the muzzle to your dog, taking it out of the box and showing it to him. Give him a treat.

3. Place the muzzle on his face and remove it IMMEDIATELY. Don't fasten it. On, off, treat. On, off, treat.

4. This time, put the muzzle on and fasten it, then give him a treat through the hole and immediately take it back off.

We need to change people's perceptions about dogs in muzzles. If a dog is wearing a muzzle in public, it doesn't mean they're dangerous. Some dogs have to wear muzzles for their own safety because they're constantly picking things up and eating them and they've been to the vet ten times. We have a dog in the day care who eats sticks and any old rubbish and has had to have three operations. He's not even remotely vicious.

# CHAPTER 6

# BREED-SPECIFIC BEHAVIOURS

What a load of old NONSENSE! I don't go by breed specifics. EVER. Out of 16,500 dogs that I've worked with, NO two of them have had the same personality.

I get *so* annoyed when people say, 'That's German Shepherds for you,' or 'Labradors are greedy. It's a Labrador thing.' ANY dog can be greedy. You hear these things all the time.

I want people to get it out of their head that it's a breed-specific thing because, number one: we're going by the dog's PERSONALITY not breed; and number two: you could have raised 30 German Shepherds and your next one will be TOTALLY different as we see in the human aggression case study in Chapter 12 with Trixie the Rottweiler. Her owners had had 12 Rottweilers before her. I hear people say it time and time again, 'We've had this breed all our lives and we've never had one like this.' And I say, 'That's because you're thinking of them as a breed but they all have INDIVIDUAL personalities.'

## Dangerous dogs

Rottweilers were the devil dog of the eighties when I was growing up. Then Pitbulls. Then XL Bullies. It's irresponsible OWNERS that are the problem, NOT the breed.

Various forms of aggression can unfortunately arise in dogs. If a dog isn't raised with love and care or feels threatened by a certain trigger, they can become aggressive. And if a dog is bred from two *fighting* dogs, then yes, WHATEVER the breed, you are likely going to have an aggressive puppy.

Aggression in dogs can be *very* dangerous, but it is FIXABLE as we see in the case studies on human aggression (Chapter 12), fear aggression (Chapter 19) and dog-on-dog aggression (Chapter 26).

## Working dogs

People buy breeds like Collies or working Cocker Spaniels and they think or are told that their unwanted behaviours are breed specific. But it's more about how far removed they are from working parents. A Collie puppy with two working dog parents, living on a farm, will need to be a working dog. That's not because of his breed but because of his *genetics*. That personality is inherently built into that dog. If you don't want a dog like that, you need to be looking at two generations or more removed from working parents.

A working Cocker that is guarding the living room and growling and snapping at the owner whenever he walks into the room, isn't doing it because he's a working Cocker Spaniel, despite what you'll read on Facebook and owners' groups. It's a dog with no mental stimulation and probably the wrong diet.

Other behaviourists will suggest 'giving him a job' or scatter-feeding because he needs to 'work'. It's got nothing to do with the breed or with him 'working'.

Instead, take it back to the POWER OF THREE and work out what your dog is lacking and sort your training plan out from there.

No more breed excuses PLEASE!

# CHAPTER 7

# SETTING YOUR OWN TRAINING GOALS

You've nailed the theory but how do you put it into practice? How do you create a training plan based on my methods that works for you and your dog at home?

Every owner that I work with has to fill in a Behaviour Questionnaire for their dog before we start training. You'll see in Part 2 that each dog has a case file with relevant sections filled out. And now it's time for you to fill out yours.

## Behaviour questionnaire

Dog's name: ........................................................................

Breed: ...............................................................................

Age: ..................................................................................

Sex: ..................................................................................

Neutered at what age: .........................................................

Where was dog acquired? .....................................................

At what age was dog acquired? .............................................

## Behavioural concerns

When did these behaviours start?..................................

Triggers?............................................................

## Dog aggression

On/off lead?.......................................................

Human aggression?..................................................

Home/in public?....................................................

What is your dog's day-to-day emotional state?

............................................................

## Previous training

Training courses attended:.........................................

1-on-1 training courses attended:..................................

## Diet

Type/brand?........................................................

No. of meals?......................................................

Food intolerances?.................................................

Treats?............................................................

When?..............................................................

How many?..........................................................

## Environment

In which areas is the dog allowed when you are at
home?..............................................................

What is the routine for you/your dog when you leave
the house?.........................................................

Where does your dog sleep?.........................................

What is your dog's reaction to owners leaving/
entering house (incl. front door)?.................................

Is your dog ever destructive/soils when left alone?

............................................................................................

Is your dog distressed when left alone?......................

Dog's reaction to visitors?...........................................

Any recent changes to household?...................................

**Mental stimulation**

Who walks the dog?.................................................

How often?...............................................................

Toys availability?..................................................

Day care?................................................................

How often?...............................................................

Other activities?....................................................

What?......................................................................

How often?...............................................................

**Key advice points to follow**

Diet:......................................................................

Environment:..........................................................

Mental stimulation:..............................................

## Be realistic

When you're setting training goals for your dog, be realistic. Using the POWER OF THREE advice from Chapter 3 – and any relevant case studies from Part 2 – think about what you could change in each of the THREE sections. Does your dog's diet need to change? How are you going to do that? Add those points to your plan. Do you need to buy safety gates? Or move your dog's bed? Does he have too much access to rooms in the house that he doesn't need? Write them down. Does your dog need more mental stimulation? How are you going to improve that? What classes might you try or what days can you plan activities and doggy play dates with friends?

I strongly recommend writing out your dog's new routine and sticking it somewhere the whole family can see, like the fridge. Remember consistency is KEY.

An ideal routine for your dog would look something like this.

## Dog's daily routine

A puppy would need a lunchtime meal as well.

### Morning
As soon as you wake up, let him out for the toilet
7–8am: Walkies
8–9am: Breakfast
10.30: Play time with toys (30–60 mins)
Training session
Quiet time

### Afternoon
2.30pm: Play time with toys (30–60 mins)
Training session
4–5pm: Dinner

### Evening
7pm: Evening walk
9pm: Last toilet trip
10–11pm: Bed time

# Part 2: Putting It into Practice

## From theory to real life

In this section of the book, we get down to brass tacks. We've had all the theory – lovely, thank you very much – but how do YOU actually fix your dog?

Over the next 20 chapters, I'll take you through a variety of different behavioural issues, from rogue recall to on-the-lead aggression, through the individual case studies and training exercises of dogs that I've fixed.

They're a motley canine crew – different breeds and ages, different issues and owners – but the thing they all have in common is that I used THE POWER OF THREE to fix them.

In every chapter you'll find helpful how tos, advice and a section on training your puppy. I want this book to be USEFUL and FUN for you AND your dog so feel free to dip in and out of chapters to get the help you need.

Whatever your challenge, we've got you covered. In clear step-by-step guides, I'll show YOU how to fix your dog.

Come with me while I go all private detective to get to the root cause of the problem. And don't worry, I'll pop in my little quips and drag queen one-liners to lighten the mood as we go.

# CHAPTER 8

# RECALL

'My dog won't come back when I let him off the lead. He runs from dog to dog, refusing to listen, adopting other families as he goes.'

Meet Max, the runaway rogue who has his owner chasing after him as he leads her on a merry dance around the dog field.

## Max's case file

**Dog's name:** Max
**Breed:** Malamute
**Age:** 3
**Sex:** Male, neutered
**Owner:** Susie

**Behavioural concerns?**
• Bad recall

**When did these behaviours start?**
• Puppy

**Previous training?**
- Treat-based reward recall approach – didn't work

**How often is Max walked?**
- 1 hour-long walk, twice per day

**What food do you feed?**
- Dry kibble
- Treats

'Put some effort in! You're not waiting for the bus!
I'm not surprised he doesn't come back to you!'

Susie had tried letting Max, the runaway Malamute, off the lead once or twice and struggled to get him back. First things first, I asked Susie to show me what she did to get Max to come back to her. In a really flat, low-energy voice she said, 'Max, come on, Max.' I thought to myself, 'We've got a right one here.' I told her, 'Put some effort in! You're not waiting for the bus! I'm not surprised he doesn't come back to you!' And then when Max didn't come back, she got frustrated, 'MAX! MAX! FOR GOD'S SAKE!' Poor Max! Being screeched at, no one's coming back for that.

With recall, it's always best to start when your dog is young but that doesn't mean you can't retrain an older dog, like Max. Good recall is important for your dog's safety, for the safety of people around him and for his mental health. But don't stress if your dog has poor recall; it's really common and I'm here to show you how to get your dog to do what you want him to do in THREE EASY STEPS.

## THE POWER OF THREE: Max's assessment

### 1. Diet
Susie was feeding Max an expensive diet thinking that was the right thing but expensive doesn't mean the best. She didn't realize it was full of carbs and hardly any meat. For dogs, carbs turn to sugar really quickly. If you have a high-energy, excitable dog, feeding him sugar is like chucking fuel on the fire. WAHEY, HE'S OFF! Nine times out of ten, in my experience, by changing his diet, you take away that excitement and high energy. We moved Max onto a raw food complete diet, twice a day, and I told Susie that she would notice a difference in Max's energy levels within three days. And sure enough she said, 'Leon, I can't believe the difference already!' because he'd calmed right down.

### 2. Environment
Susie was taking Max to a local park packed full of screaming children – absolutely crazy for an easily distracted dog like him. She was setting him up to fail. We needed somewhere without kids and with fewer distractions. You can hire dog fields by the hour in most places and these are a great starting point for a dog like Max.

### 3. Mental stimulation
A super-friendly dog like Max, who prefers to run off and play with other dogs rather than come back, is telling me that he doesn't have enough social interaction with other dogs. Most people don't understand that the less your dog is allowed to interact with others, the worse he will get. So, we put Max in a doggy day care twice a week for four weeks. Dogs are like kids – we know children thrive at school with their peers where they create independent skills, learn how to play and test what's acceptable and what's not.

---

### Max's 3-step runaway recall plan

1. Ditch the dodgy diet and replace with
a new complete raw diet, twice a day.
2. Get him some pals at doggy day care, twice a week.
3. Remedy his runaway urge via long-line
training in a safe environment.

---

## How to fix your runaway rogue's recall

Okay, let's get on with it and talk about how YOU train your dog to improve his recall.

### Dial up the energy

My job was to turn Susie into a super high-energy owner who Max thought was the bee's knees. I had my work cut out! Susie's recall just wasn't doing it. Susie was single and I said, *tongue firmly in cheek*, 'If your chat-up line is like this in a bar, I'm not surprised you're bloody single!' To get your dog to come back to you, you need bundles and bundles of excitement. Imagine what you *think* you need and then times it by a hundred. You've got to be totally OVER THE TOP, high energy, excited, proper dramatic, literally put on a Mickey Mouse voice. Dogs don't understand *what* you say but they understand your *tone* of voice. You have to be much more exciting than whatever the distraction is. It's not magic! You don't need to cover yourself in peanut butter and jam and throw yourself onto the floor to get them to come back. But you'll probably feel a right fool at first.

### Make some noise

I absolutely LOVE squeakers. They are really cheap to buy and the noise really carries so you know your dog will hear it. Sorry Max! No excuses now. Once your dog is better at recall, you won't need to jump and scream and SQUEAK-SQUEAK-SQUEAK and do backflips. But at the start I'm afraid that you do.

### Learn to love the long line

The long line is your safety net so you know you've still got control even with a tricky customer like Max. Max had a habit of attaching himself like Velcro to other families. People walked past with their dogs and Max went, 'This is my family now.' And he was off! Ungrateful sod. I used a 20–30m (65–100ft) long line which clipped to his collar, but you can use a washing line, rope, it doesn't have to be expensive. Because Max had been on the new diet for two weeks, his behaviour was better already. Susie told me that he'd normally be much more excitable.

### Call consistently

COME is a great recall command because it's direct, clear and firm. Just like me! Dogs only understand one-word commands so stop expecting him to understand a ten-minute monologue of instructions. He's switched off, love. Get your dog's attention first by calling his name and then shout 'COME!' in a high-energy voice. Remember energy, energy, energy! If you're using a squeaker, use it at the same time. You have to use the same word and technique EVERY SINGLE TIME or it will confuse him. And make sure everyone in your household – partners, kids, dog walkers – all use the same command.

### Make a BIG fuss

Always use positive reinforcement when training your dog. When they come back, give them lots of praise, make a real fuss of them for doing what you wanted and give them a high-value treat. BRING OUT THE BIG GUNS! A piece of anchovy, chicken, frankfurter or strong-smelling cheese like mature Cheddar – something they don't get all the time. A treat reinforces the connection between the command – COME – and the action we want the dog to take: to come back to us. It's not about the amount of food they're getting, it's the gesture, which I call NILFF – Nothing in Life for Free. Never punish or tell your dog off for not coming back.

### Don't be the fun police

You don't want your dog to see you as a party pooper. Once you've praised him and given him his treat for coming back, let him go again. This shows him that coming back to you doesn't stop his fun, and makes it much more likely he'll come back to you again and again. Do this a few times before you end the session and head home.

### Avoid practice overkill

Start small and build up slowly. We sent Max off (on his long line) a short distance away then gave the command COME. We did that a few times and then we gradually increased the distance and the number of distractions. We then practised in different environments until Susie was confident that Max was getting the hang of it and not just running off to play. You'll know when your dog is ready to come off the long line without you having to do backflips smeared in peanut butter. Don't over-practise recall because dogs get bored. You don't want to be practising every day – just enough to get used to the new command and routine.

### Ask 'Am I being extra enough?'

Be patient with your dog while he gets to grips with this new skill. Working slowly and consistently with him will pay off. If you have setbacks, go back to basics. Are you being EXTRA enough? Have you got high-value tasty treats? Keep your dog on the long line, use the squeaker to get him to come back, give him a super yummy treat and bundles of praise, and make sure you're sending him away again.

### How's Max doing now?

When I went back six weeks later, we took Max to the field and let him off the lead. He headed for the hills, as usual, and Susie looked at me all panicked, 'OH MY GOD, I knew this was going to happen.' I calmly told her to shout his name and say the command COME and he came straight back. It was absolutely brilliant! I smugly turned to her and said, 'They don't call me the Harry Potter of the dog world for nothing you know.' Problem solved! Susie cried tears of happiness. I love empowering people to fix their dog themselves. It's magic. Within the space of six weeks, Susie saw such a dramatic change in what Max could do and their quality of life changed MASSIVELY.

'Bring out the big guns!'

## 3 rogue recall mistakes you might be making

### 1. Running after your runaway

Don't ever run after your dog! Honestly the amount of people that do this. It drives me mad. You're making it into a game for your dog, and they'll do it more and more. Walk the opposite way, away from them. Otherwise, they learn that *you* will always go to *them*. Susie told me that if Max didn't come back to her, she chased after him, shouting and screaming in an angry voice. Jeez! A recipe for disaster!

### 2. Being the party pooper

Susie was making a really common mistake: putting Max's lead back on the minute he came back to her. That tells Max, 'Fun's over', and he won't want to come back to you next time. Better to praise and reward him, then send him away again, and repeat this a few times.

### 3. Tackling treats the wrong way

You need to reward your dog when he comes back to you, STRAIGHT AWAY, not five minutes later when he has no bloody idea what it was for and definitely not if he doesn't come back to you. This is key. He only gets the treat if you give the command COME and he comes back, not if he just runs back to you without the command. People give dogs a treat for half doing something because 'he tried' and it just confuses the dog.

### Leon's top tip

Want to be the Pied Piper of the dog field? Get a squeaker! You can buy a cheap squeaker – the inside of a soft toy – from eBay or Amazon. They're brilliant because they're small, consistent (the same sound every time), transparent (so the dog can't understand where the noise is coming from), and the high-pitched noise carries over a long distance. So even if you're low energy like Susie, your dog will want to get to where the squeaker is. Just don't blame me if hundreds of dogs come running when you use it!

### Get it right from the start: Recall training for puppies

The crucial time for teaching a puppy recall is when you first get them home. Instead, people get their puppy and they wait and wait and wait until they're a year old and then decide to try without the lead and BYEEEEE they're gone. Dogs aren't stupid! All those things they've seen in that year on the lead, they now have access to. Of course they're not sticking around. So, what should you do?

1. Start recall training from 12 weeks, right at the beginning, as soon as he's had his vaccinations and you can take him out on the lead. People are terrified to let their puppy off the lead but a dog would never run off at that age. You've just taken him from his mum and he'd be terrified if you were out of sight.
2. Take him to an enclosed area that is completely safe – a field or the beach – and away from traffic.
3. Go early in the morning, take him off the lead, and just walk and he will always follow you.
4. Introduce the command word COME and a high-value treat.

## Squirrel chasers: Recall training for dogs with a strong prey drive

If your dog loves chasing squirrels, cats or rabbits you need to teach him the word STOP.

1. Get a 'waggler' stick – a stick with rope and a toy on the end, like you see cats play with.
2. Wave it around and get your dog really excited – get him into the prey drive zone.
3. Introduce the word STOP and take the toy away and give him a treat.
4. Repeat five times. As soon as he stops, give him a treat.
5. Take the treats away. My rule is that after five times, when he understands the word, you take the treats away.

Your dog now understands the word STOP and when you're out and he goes mad chasing anything that moves you have a way of stopping him.

# CHAPTER 9

# AGGRESSION IN THE HOUSE

'My dog goes for anyone who comes to the door. I can't have visitors and I have no life.'

Jasper, the ball-breaking Jack Russell, is driving his owner mad by scaring off all her friends.

---

## Jasper's case file

**Dog's name:** Jasper
**Breed:** Jack Russell
**Age:** 7
**Sex:** Male, neutered
**Owner:** Brenda

### Behavioural concerns?
- Aggressive to visitors
- Biting

---

**When did these behaviours start?**
- Progressed from nipping
- Got worse when Brenda's partner moved out

**What food do you feed?**
- Regular kibble

## 'Jasper is CLAMPED between my legs and swinging from my jeans!'

Jasper had always been grumpy but his bad behaviour had escalated over the years – growling had turned into nipping and then to biting, with things reaching CRISIS POINT since Brenda's long-term partner had moved out.

Despite asking Brenda to keep Jasper behind the safety gate when I got there, she said, 'You see this is what he does,' and opened the gate. Thank God I had baggy jeans on that day, because normally I wear skinny jeans which look like they've been sprayed on! Jasper was CLAMPED between my legs and swinging from my jeans! I was TERRIFIED. She could have just told me what he did, I didn't need the live action show with my crown jewels in his mouth, thank you! But I'd been lucky. Jasper had bitten before, numbering the poor postman and Brenda's niece as his victims. Brenda had got to the point where she'd banned visitors from her home, removing Jasper's trigger. With no visitors, Jasper couldn't improve his social skills and Brenda's world got smaller, plunging her into loneliness and depression. Could my THREE EASY STEPS save the day?

## THE POWER OF THREE: Jasper's assessment

### 1. Diet

Jasper was eating a red meat diet – beef – full of carbs. Red meat goes hand-in-hand with aggression in dogs. We put him on a complete raw diet with chicken and salmon. We also CUT THE CARBS knowing that they turn to sugar and were causing Jasper's anxiety levels to rocket.

### 2. Environment

Brenda had installed a safety gate so Jasper couldn't get out into the hall near the front door, but he was able to hurdle over it like an Olympian! She needed to get a special high version to keep him contained.

### 3. Mental stimulation

Jasper had only ever been aggressive in the house but being a responsible owner, Brenda was worried that he might attack another dog outside so she restricted him from mixing with other dogs. He'd been getting mental stimulation from people coming into the house but that had all stopped. We needed to sort Jasper out and give him back his independence so he could be let off the lead again.

---

### Jasper's 3-step banish the biting plan

1. Cut the red meat and carbs and replace with new complete raw diet, twice a day.
2. Introduce three visitors per week alongside muzzle training.
3. Give Jasper his independence and stimulation back by exercising him safely off the lead.

## How to banish your dog's biting

Let's make a plan for how YOU deal with a dog who bites and barks.

### Ditch the co-dependency

Don't mould your life around your dog's behaviour. Brenda had banned all visitors and was horribly lonely. I had another woman who wouldn't put her oven on because she said her dog was scared of the sound of the oven so she had to microwave everything. Another couldn't put the washing machine on! It's MADNESS the hoops we jump through for our dogs. STOP! Instead of changing your normal life and behaviour, let's deal with your dog's issue.

### Don't make excuses for your dog

Dog aggression usually escalates over a period of time. Brenda had been making excuses for Jasper for years saying, 'He's grumpy.' Then after a few months of growling, he'd started nipping and pulling at clothing, and that had already escalated too far. But because she'd lived with him growling for a year, she let that go and before she knew it he was biting. Her other excuse was, 'He's being protective over me because he loves me.' Sorry to BURST YOUR BUBBLE Brenda but this kind of dog behaviour is resource-guarding. It doesn't mean Jasper loves you. He's guarding you like a toy or a piece of food. He thinks he OWNS you.

### Start on a short lead

I asked Brenda to clip a short lead onto Jasper and bring him into the living room. I had her sit down on the sofa furthest away from me. The short lead was VITAL, not just for my crown jewels but because it meant Jasper wasn't able to lunge, which would just increase his anxiety. Naturally, he went crazy when Brenda brought him in. INTRUDER ALERT! He didn't know me and Brenda belonged to him –he'd taken ownership, make no mistake!

### Ignore him

Although feisty Jasper was losing his mind, I told Brenda to just carry on chatting to me as normal. I didn't want her to acknowledge Jasper or tell him off. I told her not to pull the lead, shush him or tell him, 'Don't be silly.' Instead, completely IGNORE his behaviour. Jasper had learned that his aggressive behaviour kept people away and kept Brenda to himself. I told her, 'Jasper needs to know that his behaviour is not going to make me disappear.' Sorry Jasper, I'm not going anywhere. You're stuck with me! As soon as your dog stops barking, snarling, growling, even if it takes two hours, you've changed his behaviour.

### Meet and greet

Jasper needed his anxiety levels bringing WAAAAAYYYYY down. The best option for us to do this was by introducing him to lots of people. Luckily Brenda had a big enough support group because I needed her to bring three different people per week into the house, for the next three weeks. We made sure that none of them was in danger by keeping Jasper on a short lead and wearing a muzzle (see Chapter 5 for more detail on how to muzzle train your dog). For the first time in 18 months, visitors were going to be back in Brenda's house. I knew that Jasper would go mad at first but all Brenda had to do was what we'd done: bring him in on a short lead and chat to her friend until he stopped barking, at which point she should calmly and silently take him back behind the safety gate.

### Ditch the doggy treats

Brenda was giving Jasper a chew to keep him quiet, unknowingly rewarding his unwanted behaviour. As soon as he finished the chew, he started barking again. Jasper thought, 'She's happy with my behaviour.'

### Practise sudden movements

Once Jasper had got used to visitors being in the house, I went back and we unclipped his lead (Jasper was wearing a muzzle) and we practised me standing up and sitting down and he was as cool as could be. A nonchalant sniff of me, then he lay back down. Brenda continued to practise doing this with her friends. Don't interact with the dog in this phase – you and your visitors MUST ignore the dog, leaving him to be as relaxed as possible.

### How's Jasper doing now?

Three weeks later Jasper was a changed dog. He'd gone from being a dog swinging off my denim with anxiety, to one who barely noticed I was there. There was no yapping at the front door and when Brenda brought him into the living room in his muzzle, he couldn't have been less interested in my crotch if he tried. He didn't even bark, he just sat there. She'd put boundaries in place and had been consistent. Yay Brenda! Within three months, visitors were able to come and go and within five months, the muzzle was totally off with no fear of attack. 'You've given me back my independence,' Brenda said, hugging me. It just goes to show, you don't need to adapt your life to a dog's behavioural problem – you can just solve the problem, full stop. Jasper ended up loving the visitors.

'He couldn't have been less interested in my crotch.'

### 3 mistakes that might be upping your dog's aggression

**1. Accidentally rewarding your dog**
Do you tell your dog off for aggressive behaviour? For some dogs, even telling them off is seen as a reward because they have your full – albeit negative – attention.

**2. Feeding red meat**
Any red meat – beef, lamb, rabbit – will increase your dog's aggression. Move them to fish or white meat and see them calm down.

**3. Watch your tone of voice**
If you're using a sympathetic tone of voice to tell your dog off, they will think you're rewarding them. Be firm and fair. And keep it to one-word commands rather than sentences, especially with unwanted behaviour, so your dog can understand.

> ### Leon's top tip
>
> Create red zones in your home; these are no-go dog zones.
> The door is a hot spot – it's where people are coming in and leaving,
> so if your dog has an issue with guarding, biting or aggression at
> the door, they shouldn't be in the hallway in the first place.
> You're setting them up to fail. A dog should never be in a red zone
> area. It's a hot spot and what is a hot spot not? A good spot!

## Biting back: How to prevent your puppy biting

Some puppy-training books advise using a chew to divert your puppy when he is mouthing you. But this is completely wrong because you're REWARDING the chewing behaviour. It should be a firm but fair NO in an authoritative voice. When you say NO your puppy will look at you, make eye contact with you, and still keep his mouth on your hand. It's another authoritative NO directly at him and you'll find that he will release. It's completely normal for it to be the second NO that works rather than the first.

## Neutering: When to make the call

We look at neutering in detail in Chapter 5 but when a dog is maturing – up to 18 months – their hormones are all over the place, like a teenager going through puberty. Testosterone or the female equivalent, oestrogen, is a dog's only source of confidence. Take away their equipment, stopping the production of those hormones, and you've got a dog like Jasper not only with behavioural issues, but no confidence either, which equals a very scared dog indeed. Perhaps poor Jasper had gone for my crown jewels in a fit of envy at losing his own?

# CHAPTER 10

# FEAR OF LOUD NOISES

'My dog is super anxious and terrified of loud noises so fireworks are hell for him.'

Anxious Alfie hates loud noises and is a nervous wreck in the house, barking at everything all the time out of fear.

## Alfie's case file

**Dog's name:** Alfie
**Breed:** Pug
**Age:** 4
**Sex:** Male, neutered
**Owner:** Kerry

### Behavioural concerns?
- Fear of loud noises
- Barking at everything

### When did these behaviours start?
- Puppy

**Previous training?**
- None

**What food do you feed?**
- Dry biscuits with beef

### 'BANISH THE BEEF!'

Alfie, the anxious pug, was barking MAD, driving owner Kerry to absolute distraction. She needed help and FAST! Alfie was barking at anything that moved. Noises that weren't even there. There was poor Kerry thinking she's got a poltergeist! FETCH THE HOLY WATER! She was convinced that he was doing it for attention, 'I can't hear anything. He's doing it on purpose.' Although Alfie seemed to be terrified of everything, firework celebrations were absolute hell for him. Shaking, being sick, diarrhoea, AWFUL. The ultimate stress.

Alfie had had a particularly bad time because Kerry had thrown a Halloween and fireworks bash for all the kids in the neighbourhood. There were candles in pumpkins scattered around, a paddling pool full of water in the middle of the living room for apple bobbing, and the total chaos that comes of twenty kids in costume running riot. At some point in the night, Alfie was running round barking and strayed too close to a candle and singed his tail. In a panic, Kerry dunked him in the paddling pool in the middle of all these kids. He wasn't seriously harmed but he was emotionally traumatized. The poor dog needed THERAPY!

Dogs that are scared of loud noises and fireworks, like Alfie, suffer all year round because every event is celebrated with a sky rocket and a side of sparklers now! New Year's Eve! Weddings! Birthdays! A random Tuesday in March! GET THE FIREWORKS OUT! Honestly! Dogs that are scared of fireworks are showing FEAR but they're also showing SENSORY OVERLOAD. There's too much going on – flashing, colourful lights, GROUND-SHAKING bangs, fizzes and pop-pop-pops. IT'S LIKE A WAR ZONE! Dogs can hear higher frequency noises than humans and they can hear sounds that are further away than we can so when we think it's bad, it's total hell for dogs. Dogs don't always bark to show they are scared – they might show it by a racing heart, shaking, drooling or pacing. It's SO important to desensitize your dog to fireworks and loud noises. Here's how in THREE SIMPLE STEPS.

## THE POWER OF THREE: Alfie's assessment

### 1. Diet

Anxious Alfie was on a dry food biscuit diet with beef. Any red meat for dogs with anxiety issues is a big NO-NO! It's packed FULL of testosterone. Alfie's biscuits also had lots of carbohydrate (brown rice, potatoes, barley) which turns to sugar for a dog. AGAIN NO! Giving an anxious dog sugar is making the situation a hundred times worse. We BANISHED THE BEEF and moved him onto a raw chicken and turkey complete dog food which I knew would almost instantly lower his energy levels and his anxiety.

### 2. Environment

Alfie's house was a lesson in sensory overload. I've never been anywhere so busy and chaotic. Times Square would be more relaxing! I had a headache the moment I walked in. It was like a drop-in centre for neighbourhood kids, with six children roaming around at any time. They were shouting over each other, the TV was on full blast. PASS THE PAINKILLERS! And to add insult to injury, anxious Alfie's bed was right in the middle of all the chaos. Poor Alfie. The first thing I did was get Kerry to move Alfie's bed to the kitchen, away from all the noise so he could have his own personal space. We created a cosy bed in a crate and put a safety gate up to keep unwanted visitors OUT. I call a spade a spade and I told Kerry, 'This is YOUR house and you need to put some boundaries in place. All this screaming and shouting is not a nice environment for a dog!'

## 3. Mental stimulation

We took Alfie for a walk. It was chaos, he was looking everywhere, EYES OUT ON STALKS, barking at EVERYTHING – people, cars, birds, children. He was going crazy. It was IMMEDIATELY clear to me what was going on. Kerry was letting him into the backyard for the toilet and that was it. No walks. We'd just exposed him to an outside world that he had NO knowledge about. You could see the terror in his face. He'd never had the visuals to match the noises he could hear from inside the house and this TOTALLY explained why he was so noise sensitive.

### Alfie's 3-step plan for fuss-free fireworks

1. Banish the beef! Swap it out for a new chicken and turkey complete raw diet, twice a day.
2. Create a quiet, safe space away from the chaos for doggy down time.
3. Desensitization to loud noises to slowly and safely reduce Alfie's anxiety.

### How to fix firework fear

Okay, let's chat about how YOU train your dog for a fuss-free fireworks night.

### Start earlier than you think

Most people don't start thinking about Bonfire Night, 4th of July, Diwali or New Year's Eve until a week or two, or even the day, before. That's TOO LATE! In an ideal situation, you should be preparing your dog SIX MONTHS before any of these events.

### Dedicate time to doggy desensitization

Desensitize your dog to sound in a kind and loving way. YouTube is a great resource for all different kinds of noises – from fireworks to traffic, to motorbikes. Start the volume on the very lowest setting. You won't be able to hear it but I guarantee your dog WILL! I did this with Kerry. We couldn't hear anything but Alfie's ears were twitching on high alert. Dogs' ears are much more sensitive than ours. An hour or two per day, when you're sitting watching TV, just have it on in the background so he can hear it.

### Take your time

Build up the volume slowly – start with the lowest volume and increase it by 0.5 on the volume each week. This means you will desensitize your dog to the sound but also to the volume. Fireworks are INSANELY loud so it's no good just desensitizing him to really quiet ones. Imagine how loud actual fireworks are for dogs. You need to build it up to the point where your dog can sit in the living room and hear fireworks at their normal volume like nothing is going on. For Alfie it took two weeks to get to the stage of being fine with fireworks at a low level with Kerry just able to hear it. But this was MAJOR progress for these two!

### Light the way

You can also do light desensitization on YouTube. There are videos of low-key fireworks, not massively bright or strobing. They're much slower. Put the video on your TV screen, for ten minutes in the morning and ten minutes in the afternoon. That way if he has to go outside to the toilet or sees the odd flash of different colours, you've prepared him for it.

### Make a doggy den

Build your dog a small, secure den to help him feel safe. If you don't have a crate for your dog, you can use the space behind the sofa. The smaller the space, the more secure he'll feel. Let your inner interior designer OUT and drape blankets over it, like you would if you were making a den for a child. Put some of his favourite toys in there. Close your curtains and blinds. The different flashes of light and different colours can be as distressing as the loud noises. I CANNOT STAND big overhead lights so I always have a lamp on. Make it feel cosy but don't sit in the dark.

### Make fireworks fuss-free

Carry on as normal, do the stuff you would normally do – make dinner, watch TV, read a book. Let your dog decide where he wants to be. We make decisions based on what we think is best for the dog – sitting on your knee, in silence, in the dark – NO. Put him DOWN! You're stopping him having the freedom to go where HE feels safe and comfortable. We want to comfort our dogs but it's FAR worse to mollycoddle your dog, stroking him, telling him he's fine, forcing him to sit on your knee. You are actually making his anxiety WORSE when you do that.

### Turn the telly down

People say put your TV or radio on really loud. That's a TERRIBLE idea. It's just heaping sensory overload on top of sensory overload. DO THE OPPOSITE. We already know that dogs can hear fireworks even if we can't. Having fireworks + a blaring TV + a deafening radio = a TOTALLY freaked-out dog.

### Just say NO!

I would only use tranquillizers as a last resort if nothing else works (as tempting as they might be for ALL OF US when confronted with the stress of very loud noises). Instead, try a thunder vest. These are drug-free and work on a similar principle to swaddling a baby or using a weighted blanket – they provide a gentle, constant pressure. We're drugging a lot of dogs that don't need it.

### Stay put

Put the sparklers DOWN. Step away from the Roman candle. Don't be tempted to pop out to a fireworks show or a New Year's Eve party and leave your dog alone with the telly playing full blast. It's not fair. You need to be there to support him and keep him SAFE.

### Tackle his treats

Treats such as gravy bones are full of sugar. When dogs have been on a raw food diet for two weeks, I get their owners to give them a regular treat and see how it affects them. They're BOUNCING OFF THE WALLS. I'd give them fresh shredded chicken if you're giving them a treat. Pop the chicken or a chew in their crate or den to encourage them to use it.

### How's Alfie doing now?

When I went back to see Alfie, he was a TOTALLY DIFFERENT dog. He was perfectly socialized, confident, going for regular walks and interacting with other dogs in the park. Kerry pulled it together and once it was pointed out to her, even though it was BLATANTLY obvious to me, she understood. I said, 'You can stand here and blame yourself all you like. That's not what I'm here for, I'm here to resolve the situation.' She had set boundaries, not only with Alfie but in the household, so her home was a much calmer, nicer environment for everyone to live in.

'The smaller the space, the more secure he'll feel.'

## 3 mistakes that can make your dog's fear of loud noises worse

### 1. Over-compensating
No one likes to see their dog scared, but if you insist on him being on your knee, making a huge fuss every time he hears a bang, you're reinforcing the idea that he has something to be scared of.

### 2. Taking him outside to see what he's scared of
I get the theory, that if he just *sees* the fireworks, he might not be so scared. But no, you're making things worse. Keep him inside, give him his space, stay calm.

### 3. Trying to mask the noise
The danger of putting the radio and TV on FULL BLAST to drown out the fireworks is that your dog will have sensory OVERLOAD. He'll still hear the fireworks but now he's also losing it because of all the other noise.

> **Leon's top tip**
>
> If you have a noise-sensitive dog, always check with the
> vet if your dog has got an ear infection. Check there's nothing
> in his ear canal or a yeast infection in his ears. They are
> very common in dogs and can increase noise sensitivity.

### It's not just fireworks: Stamp out traffic terror

Some dogs are TERRIFIED of traffic – lorries, buses, motorbikes, bicycles, bin trucks – you name it. We cover this in detail in Chapter 27. It's tempting to just avoid places where your dog will come into contact with those things but you never know when a motorbike could whizz past. You and your dog deserve better! Instead, slowly desensitize your dog to scary noises. Take him out for a short walk (15 minutes) first thing in the morning at 7am, before the kids are going to school, when there's traffic but not too much. And again last thing before it gets dark. Do this twice a day for two weeks. This will expose him to general sounds and traffic. Then move your morning walk a bit later and your evening walk a bit earlier so it's a bit busier, and so on, until he's happy with all sorts going on. Slowly increase your walking time too so that you're out for longer.

### Avoid anxiety from the start: Puppy training

Puppies need to be PROPERLY socialized up to the age of 16 weeks.

1. Socialize your puppy in your arms before he's had all his vaccinations, and on the ground once he has.
2. Make a list of places and things you need to show your puppy and tick them off. Stand outside the supermarket on a busy Saturday morning, walk past a school just as the children are being released at the end of the day, stand at a bus stop. You get the idea. This way they don't build up the fear that Alfie had because he'd never experienced these things.

3. Don't think the best way to make sure your puppy isn't scared of fireworks is to take them to a fireworks event. 'Look Geoffrey, little Peanut is barking at his favourite firework!' NO. That's the one that traumatized him the most.

## Have you got an Anxious Alfie?

### Older dogs
As soon as you see any sign that your dog has an issue with a specific sound, do sound desensitization IMMEDIATELY. Don't just avoid the sound. With the best will in the world you can't control the sounds outside your home. You don't know when a bin lorry is going to come rattling past or a motorbike will whizz by. Using diversion or avoidance techniques is not fixing the problem. It needs to be fixed in a safe, controlled environment.

### Rehomed dogs
If you have a rescue dog, you should get a full breakdown of any issues he has from the rehoming centre – a list of what he likes and doesn't like. That DOESN'T mean you should avoid them, it just means you need to be more considerate, careful and plan more for THOSE noises.

# CHAPTER 11

# DOGGY DISOBEDIENCE

'My dog does what she likes, when she likes, with total disregard for me. How can I make her listen and behave herself?'

Doggy diva Betty is a fun-loving, table-dancing showgirl with bad manners.

---

## Betty's case file

**Dog's name:** Betty
**Breed:** Beagle
**Age:** 2
**Sex:** Female, spayed
**Owner:** Simone

**Behavioural concerns?**
- Dancing on the dining room table
- Ignoring her owner

**When did these behaviours start?**
- Puppy

---

> **What food do you feed?**
> - Dry dog biscuits with only 2 per cent meat

## 'If she was auditioning for Moulin Rouge she'd pass with flying colours. But she's not!'

Betty the Beagle was running up and down the dinner table, tip-tapping along, when I first met her and owner Simone. I said, 'What's going on here?' and Simone said, 'Oh it's fine, just ignore her. She doesn't eat anything off the plates.' ERRR, HOLD ON ONE SECOND! Would you let a three-year-old child run up and down here? LOOK AT HER! She was tap-dancing like a Broadway showgirl. If she was auditioning for Moulin Rouge she'd pass with flying colours. But she's not! She was running up and down the dinner table and all Simone could say was, 'She's not eating the food.' She shouldn't have been up there in the first place! I wound myself up into a frenzy. She wasn't even being naughty. She was just doing what she wanted because she'd not been told any different. I had to sort this DOGGY DIVA out! *jazz hands*

### THE POWER OF THREE: Betty's assessment

#### 1. Diet
Simone was feeding Betty a low-quality dog food without realizing. It only had 2 per cent meat in it (when it should have been higher), but overall, it wasn't contributing to Betty's bad behaviour. We changed her diet to a healthier raw food.

#### 2. Environment
Simone had a lovely house and Betty was just going crazy, skidding across the wooden floors like it was her own personal ice rink, then getting on the table like it was a West End stage, having a lovely little time. Simone was retired,

totally doting on Betty, who was able to do what she liked, when she liked. This was a house with no boundaries, consistency, routine, NOTHING. Betty was pulling clothes off the ironing pile and hiding them around the room. I told Simone, 'She's piecing together her next showgirl costume!'

## 3. Mental stimulation

Betty was spoiled rotten. It was clearly obvious Simone let her do whatever she wanted to do. She'd made that VERY CLEAR. Simone walked her every day and she had about a thousand toys – I've seen fewer stuffed animals in a kids' toy shop – but they were out ALL THE TIME. Simone was providing everything for Betty, except the one thing Betty needed: a parental role model.

---

### Betty's 3-step doggy disobedience plan

1. Replace the unhealthy diet with new complete raw food, twice a day.
2. Give Betty some firm boundaries and routine.
3. Teach our showgirl some manners.

---

## How to fix your doggy diva

If your dog is running riot like Betty, here's how YOU can train your dog to behave better.

### Ring in a new routine

We needed to talk routines, but not the dancing kind that Betty might be familiar with! *Back in your dressing room Betty!* I asked Simone to create a timetable for Betty from Monday to Sunday, blocking out mornings, afternoons and evenings. She needed routine and structure, not something different every day. Betty would bark when SHE decided she wanted to get up each day. Poor Simone! Some days that was 5am, other days it was 8am.

We needed to set her wake up time, feed times, toilet times, walk times and play times, and the rest would fall into place allowing Betty to start reacting to her own body clock.

### Establish set meal times

It's important for your diva to have set meal times. The ideal time to feed your dog is 8–9am every day AFTER you've walked them. I recommend two feeds per day. Their dinner should be no later than 5pm, if you're going to bed around 10–11pm. That way she can have her final walk and toilet and you can go to bed knowing she's comfortable and can have a lovely night's sleep. Not all dogs like eating at breakfast and that's fine, just feed them in the evening or afternoon instead.

### Make meal times a red-carpet event

You need to make food time an exciting, positive experience. ROLL OUT THE RED CARPET. When your dog gets up in the morning, she needs something to look forward to. What do dogs have in their lives? They have you, food, play time and exercise. Never leave dog food on the floor if your dog doesn't eat it. If you take away their drive for food, if it's left down all day, you can easily get a depressed dog on your hands. Also, don't be tempted to just top your dog's bowl up whenever they eat a bit. Owners who do this have ZERO idea how much food their dog is eating in a 24-hour period. It's really bad for your dog's health.

### Make sure your dog has a Lights, camera, ACTION-packed day

Make time every day to play with your dog. Mid-morning and mid-afternoon, schedule a 30–60 minute play time where you get the toy box out and interact with her. When you've finished, pop her toys away and have some quiet, relaxing time. WHERE you play with your dog is really important. Certain rooms should be used for certain things. Your dog doesn't understand if you have play time in the living room in the morning, then it's not play time again in there when you're wanting to watch your Scandi crime drama of an evening. She'll keep dropping her ball at your feet and driving you MAD.

## Don't spoil her

Spoiling your dog might make *you* feel good but it won't be making *her* feel so great. Simone was treating Betty the same way she treated her three-year-old granddaughter when she visited. Grandparents always spoil kids. I do it with my grandsons. I'm much softer on them than I ever was with my own kids. But dogs need balance and boundaries. If she doesn't have them, she won't understand what's expected of her and she'll go into freefall and it can cause a massive storm of issues and behavioural problems.

## Teach that diva some manners

In order to get Betty off the table tops, we had to teach her the word UP so she could understand the opposite, OFF. To teach UP, I used my hands and patted my chest and said UP. So, we had hand movement, a noise (patting your chest) and the verbal command. You should be able to take any one of those away once she understands it. I call it DOGGY SIGN LANGUAGE. If I'm hitting my chest, the dog knows to jump up. Once she'd jumped up, we gave her a treat, ten times maximum. As soon as she had learned that word, I got her UP and I didn't give her a treat and I pointed to the side and said OFF. As I said OFF, I took half a step back so that naturally she came to the floor without any physical interaction. Then I gave her a treat.

## Reward CORRECT behaviour

Some people give their dog a treat if they jump off and back up, or take one leg off. NO! Your dog should only get a treat when she does it properly. There's no in between. I'd do that a maximum of ten times. Then that is it. No more treats. This is a mistake a lot of people make. They teach their dog a command and then they ruin it by continuing to give them a treat. If you're giving her a treat for every UP, she'll jump up on stuff, waiting for her treat. And if you give her a treat for OFF, she'll still jump up in order to jump off and get the treat. This is how we end up being TREAT-DRIVEN with doggy divas. It's over-rewarding.

### How's Betty doing now?

Betty's problem was all about structure, routine and consistency. Once we'd sorted that out, I knew she'd be fine. Betty is absolutely perfect now. No more table dancing. She's hung up her tap shoes like a washed-up old showgirl. She has a (non-dancing) routine now for the rest of her life.

### 'Betty has hung up her tap shoes!'

## Doggy Diva Timetable

### Morning
As soon as you wake up, let her out for the toilet
7–8am: Walkies
8–9am: Breakfast
10.30: Play time with toys (30–60 mins)
Quiet time

### Afternoon
2.30pm: Play time with toys (30–60 mins)
5pm: Dinner

### Evening
7pm: Evening walk
9pm: Last toilet trip
10–11pm: Bed time

## 3 doggy diva mistakes you might be making

### 1. Not leaving space between your commands

Give your dog space between your commands. I hear people saying, 'UP-UP-UP-UP'. Breathe! Say your command. Pause. Let her make the decision. Give her the time and chance to think. You can see dogs thinking, processing it. 'What do they want me to do now?' Allow them to find their way.

### 2. Not using positive reinforcement

We ALWAYS want to be using positive reinforcement when training our dogs, not punishing them for unwanted behaviour. Be firm and clear and reward her when she gets it right.

### 3. Not having clear boundaries

Does your dog definitely know what behaviour you expect from her? A lot of dogs are dismissed as 'naughty' when actually they've never been shown anything different. If you let your little showgirl tip-tap on the table, you can't get cross with her for doing it!

## Leon's top tip

People have an obsession with giving their dogs treats throughout the day. These dogs get about 15 treats a day for doing ABSOLUTELY NOTHING. 'Oh, aren't you cute? Here, have a treat. Oh, you just had a little drink! Here, have a treat.' IT'S GOT TO STOP! I ask people to put the treat in a jar every time they're tempted to give it to their dog and they're always shocked by how many are in there, just from complete habit – they're not even aware they're doing it. They're thinking, 'Why is my dog getting so fat!?' Keep the treats out of sight, out of mind. If they're out on the counter top, you'll keep dipping in and before you know it, they've had 17 packs of gravy bones in a week!

## Get it right from the start: Diva training for puppies

It's never too late to teach a dog a command but it's always best to start them young.

1. Teach your puppy SIT, STAY, COME, UP and OFF and make it a game for them.
2. Be clear and concise, firm but fair.
3. Use an authoritative voice and one-word commands.
4. Be consistent.

CHAPTER 12

# HUMAN AGGRESSION

'My dog has started attacking me out of the blue. Help!'

Trixie, the tyrant Rotty, has her owner living in fear for her safety.

## Trixie's case file

**Dog's name:** Trixie
**Breed:** Rottweiler
**Age:** 3
**Sex:** Female, spayed
**Owner:** Jackie

### Behavioural concerns?

- Aggressive to owner

### When did these behaviours start?

- 6 weeks after rehoming

**Previous history?**
- Growling at strangers
- Guarding toys
- Lunging

**What food do you feed?**
- Red meat diet

'There's always a reason why a dog is
"human aggressive". ALWAYS.'

Jackie and husband Trevor had rehomed Trixie six weeks earlier and out of nowhere one day Trixie had attacked her. Over the last 20 years, Jackie and Trevor had adopted 12 other Rottweilers. They had experience, knew the breed, everything. Finding themselves without a dog, they'd adopted Trixie from a rescue centre. She had multiple behavioural issues, growling and lunging at strangers, but they were able to deal with all of her issues, due to their wealth of experience. However, things changed OVERNIGHT. It was like a switch. Jackie had stood up to go to the toilet and Trixie had launched herself at Jackie, biting her arm and trying to rag her. Jackie screamed, which made Trixie jump and run back over to her bed as if nothing had happened.

Understandably, Jackie was TERRIFIED. She left it a while and then tried again but the exact same thing happened. She was in the house alone, unable to move for EIGHT HOURS, sitting in her own urine, until her husband got home from work. AWFUL! Jackie desperately wanted to keep Trixie but she wanted to know WHAT WAS GOING ON. She knew that Trixie would have been put to sleep if she'd been sent back to the rehoming centre. There's always a reason why a dog is 'human aggressive'. ALWAYS. They needed help – AND FAST! – to save this beautiful, bouncy, soppy Rottweiler, and her lovely owners, from an awful fate.

## THE POWER OF THREE: Trixie's assessment

### 1. Diet
Jackie was feeding Trixie a 100 per cent beef diet. Because she'd had issues in the past – growling at new people and being possessive of her toys – it was important to reduce her red meat intake, which was only AMPLIFYING her aggression.

### 2. Environment
Jackie had been diagnosed with multiple sclerosis (MS) just before she got Trixie but it had deteriorated at a rapid pace. Jackie explained to me that she now needed to use a Zimmer frame to get up out of her chair. LIGHT-BULB MOMENT. It was Jackie's Zimmer frame that was causing Trixie to attack her. She was reacting through FEAR aggression causing her to lunge at Jackie. Dogs can't deal with strange movement. So, for Trixie to see Jackie suddenly shuffling along on her Zimmer frame, she was immediately on the defence. This poor woman – she had just been diagnosed with a debilitating disease and now she was getting attacked by her dog. Can you imagine?

### 3. Mental stimulation
Because Trixie had been possessive of her toys in her previous home, I advised Jackie to keep toys in a toy box and bring them out for 45 minutes of play time each day with her.

## Trixie's 3-step anger management plan

1. Swap out aggression-inducing red meat for chicken or turkey raw complete diet, twice a day.
2. Do muzzle training to help fix the problem.
3. Turn Trixie's trigger into something positive.

## How to fix your combative canine

If you have a dog that's aggressive in the house, it is *really* important that you fix the issue before anyone gets hurt. Let's look at the steps you can take to sort your dog's bullying tactics.

## Put a muzzle on her

I only ever use a muzzle to rehabilitate a dog. It is NOT a permanent fix and when I hear people talking about muzzles in a negative way, I explain that it's only a *bad* thing if it isn't introduced the correct way or it's used as punishment. I use a FOUR-STEP METHOD (see below). Yes, your dog might look a bit like Hannibal Lector (pass the Chianti!) but we needed Trixie and Jackie to be in a safe environment where Jackie was able to stand up using her frame. When a dog bites, they get a positive sensation, which is hard to explain, but it's satisfying for them. The muzzle modifies this behaviour because when Trixie launched herself at Jackie, the muzzle bashed against her nose so she was no longer able to clamp on and get that sensory fix.

## Stay calm as the red mist descends

EASY FOR ME TO SAY! I explained to Jackie that when she got up, even with the muzzle on, Trixie was going to come BOUNDING over from the other side of the room and launch herself at her. Although this was scary, Jackie could take comfort in knowing that Trixie couldn't hurt her when she was wearing the muzzle so that would stop any nervous energy coming off Jackie. And sometimes that alone can change a dog's behaviour. I asked Jackie to carry on as normal, getting up to go to the bathroom and to repeat the process until Trixie stopped reacting.

### Desensitize your dog to the trigger

With the muzzle on Trixie, Jackie got up to use her Zimmer frame and Trixie jumped up, launched at her, but didn't get that impact sensory fix. Jackie did it again, and the same thing happened. And then the behaviour stopped. It was UNBELIEVABLE! Twice!

### Turn Trixie's trigger from negative to positive

Once we were confident that Jackie could safely get up and use her frame to move around the house without Trixie reacting, we removed the muzzle and did the same thing, with Jackie getting up and using her frame. When Trixie didn't react, Jackie gave her a treat. She did this over and over. Once the trigger – Jackie's shuffling movement – was turned from a negative experience to a positive experience with the treats, Trixie happily slept in her bed while Jackie went in and out of the room.

### How's Trixie doing now?

When I first met them, Jackie's world had been turned upside down with her MS diagnosis and then dealing with Trixie's aggression. Trixie was reacting naturally because Jackie was making strange movements she hadn't seen before but once the trigger was found and we got it sorted, that was it. JOB DONE! She's been fine ever since.

### 'ALL dogs can be rehabilitated!'

## 3 common mistakes you might be making with your cranky canine

### 1. Making excuses for your big bully
People try to justify their dog's aggression. 'I got up too quickly, it was my fault, I did this or that.' Or 'He's just protecting me/his toys/his food.' DO NOT validate your grouchy dog's behaviour. It will escalate and get worse if you don't deal with it now.

### 2. Under-exercising your dog
A dog with too much energy can cause conflict. We only take dogs into the day care weekly, not once a fortnight, because their energy is too high. If they're bursting with energy, BOUNCING OFF THE WALLS, the other dogs are saying, 'What the hell are you doing? BACK OFF!'

### 3. Not treating your dog as an individual
Every dog has their own personality. You might have rescued or had dogs for years. You could have rescued 50 dogs before, but they're *all* different. You can have all the experience in the world and still have issues.

## Leon's top tip

Dogs don't just attack for no reason – they might have experienced abuse from a human or they've been rehomed, like Trixie, and they've already got issues. You need to figure out their TRIGGER. Think about exactly what happened before the dog attacked. Did someone stand up fast? Did they move their legs or wave their arms? The trigger could be a hand or foot. That tells me they've been abused in the past or suffered physical trauma whether by accident or on purpose. I went to see a Collie who was attacking people's feet. It turned out the husband had kicked the dog when he was drunk and the dog was now terrified of feet!

## Breed-specific behaviour

As we discuss in Chapter 6, banning a certain breed doesn't solve the problem. This issue was caused by a trigger, NOT a breed-specific behaviour. Because Trixie is a Rottweiler, that's all Jackie had been told – that she was attacking her BECAUSE she was a Rotty. Rottweilers were the DEVIL DOG of the Eighties. I believe that breed is TOTALLY IRRELEVANT in every case. ALL dogs can be rehabilitated. If I can rehabilitate a dog that has been bred to kill, then I can rehabilitate any dog. Euthanasia is not the answer.

## Get it right from the start: Avoiding aggression in puppies

A lot of aggression is about resource-guarding where your dog sees something as *theirs* and theirs alone and they guard it.

1. Start as you mean to go on. I'm strict on this. If your puppy won't let go of a toy, and is growling or nipping, you must NOT give her a treat or a chew to get her to let go because it's rewarding the unwanted behaviour. It will create a MONSTER.
2. Don't EVER give a dog food as a diversion to stop her doing something you don't want her to do. Diversion techniques are not a way of dealing with aggression. But 99 per cent of people are told that if their puppy is pulling at their clothes or nipping them, to give them a chew stick to divert them.
3. Don't shout at your puppy – they may see this as a reward – they got your ATTENTION even if it was negative attention.

## Muzzle training

In Chapter 5, we cover muzzle training in more detail but I use FOUR PHASES. Remember muzzles are only a *temporary* solution to help fix threatening behaviour. They are NEVER to be used as punishment. Make sure the muzzle you pick is kind, impossible to remove and safe. I like ones that have a gap at the bottom so the dog can eat and drink but can't bite. They're not restricted in any way other than not being able to bite.

**Phase 1:** Get the muzzle and keep it in the box. Fill the box with frankfurters or Cheddar cheese – something high value with a really strong smell. I've even used blue cheese before – pass the port and crackers! It works BRILLIANTLY. The idea is that the dog sees the box and the muzzle for the very first time and it is a positive experience. So many people get a muzzle, take it out of the box, shove it on their dog's face and then wonder why they're trying to get it off. Well yeah! I'm not surprised they don't like it! WOULD YOU? If you mess that first introduction up, you will have to buy another muzzle in a different colour.

**Phase 2:** Introduce the muzzle to your dog, taking it out of the box and showing it to her.

**Phase 3:** Place the muzzle on her face and remove it immediately. Don't fasten it. On, off, treat. On, off, treat.

**Phase 4:** This time, put the muzzle on and fasten it, then give her the treat through the hole and immediately take it back off.

Now your dog is ready.

# CHAPTER 13

# STEALING FOOD

'My dog scoffs our food before we get a look in! Uncooked roast dinner? Gone! Our daughter's birthday cake, complete with candles? Down the hatch!'

Meet Murphy, the greedy German Shepherd, who just can't say no to food.

## Murphy's case file

**Dog's name:** Murphy
**Breed:** German Shepherd
**Age:** 4
**Sex:** Male, neutered
**Owners:** Kelly, Keith and daughter, Sophie

## Behavioural concerns?
• Stealing food

## When did these behaviours start?
• Puppy

**Previous training?**
• Telling him to get off but using different words:
Off, Down, Get off, Leave it, Don't you dare, No.
Hadn't worked

**What food do you feed?**
• Dry kibble

> 'He stole – and ate – Sophie's surprise
> birthday cake including the box and the candles!
> And ended up pooping glitter!'

Food-obsessed Murphy was a dog with an unhealthy appetite. This dog thought every day was an ALL-YOU-CAN-EAT BUFFET! When I first met Murphy, Kelly put some bread at the back of the work surface, and as soon as her back was turned Murphy popped up like a seal out of the sea. And SNATCHED it. Murphy wasn't fussy: bread, pies, an entire raw chicken carcass. He ate it completely raw. AND he could also open the fridge. He'd push his long nose into the rubber seal and pull backwards. I'd never seen *anything* like it. They put a child lock on the fridge but he could still open it! He'd help himself WHENEVER he liked. But when Murphy ate their eight-year-old daughter Sophie's surprise unicorn birthday cake, including the number 8 candle, and their house was covered in glitter poop, they knew they had to get help.

## THE POWER OF THREE: Murphy's assessment

### 1. Diet
The first thing a lot of people with dogs who steal food ask is, 'Are they getting fed enough?' He was on a dry biscuit diet but this issue wasn't ANYTHING

to do with his diet. For his health and wellbeing, I put him on a raw chicken diet to make sure he was getting all his nutrients, and I included full-fat goats' milk for Kelly to pour over his raw food. It contains essential fatty acids so it was good for his joints as he is a large-breed dog. Dogs can get digestive issues from the lactose in dairy but goats' milk has 12 per cent less lactose than cow's milk, making it easier to digest.

## 2. Environment

THIS was the problem. Murphy had FULL access to the kitchen. He was in there whenever the family were cooking, whenever the fridge door was open, he was there sticking his long nose in. Whenever anything was going on in the kitchen, Murphy was THERE! He could see where everything was going. They'd bring the shopping in and he'd be cataloguing where it was being put – 'I'll have those sausages later. Oh cake, my favourite!' Because he was so tall, he didn't even need to jump up on work tops. He just licked along the side. NOT VERY HYGIENIC! His easy access made him OBSESSED with food.

## 3. Mental stimulation

Murphy had a full social life, going to day care once a week because Keith was away a lot. He had lots of doggy pals and he was getting plenty of walks and play time. His family were doing everything right.

---

### Murphy's 3-step greed-gobbling plan

1. Swap out dry biscuits for a nutrient-rich raw complete diet topped off with full-fat goats' milk to help his bones.
2. Continue at doggy day care and schedule regular play times.
3. Curb his over-eating by reducing his access to the kitchen.

### How to fix your greedy glutton

Stealing food is all about ACCESS. Some dogs, like humans, have no OFF switch and will eat and eat and eat. Why have one biscuit when you could have three packets? They never feel full. Let's look at how YOU can train your dog to reduce their snack obsession.

### Ban your canine from the kitchen

The first and most important thing was to BAN Murphy from his favourite place: the kitchen. He was not Gordon Ramsay – he didn't need to be in there! We fixed a high safety gate so he couldn't jump over it. For a lot of owners, it doesn't enter their head that their dog doesn't need to be in the kitchen, but you wouldn't have a three-year-old child toddling around when you've got pans bubbling over or when you're lifting your roast dinner out of the hot oven, would you? It's DANGEROUS.

### Supervise so they can't steal

If your dog's crate is in the kitchen or you feed your dog in there, that's absolutely *fine*. But he needs to be SUPERVISED. He shouldn't just be wandering around like a shoplifter casing the place. Dogs get fed twice a day and it takes five minutes so you can do that under supervision and then usher them back out before they manage to stuff half a chicken and a pack of sausages into their chops! If your dog sleeps in the kitchen with no crate, then I'd advise moving their sleeping place somewhere else.

### Retrain your ravenous beast

Open-plan living can make safety gates a tricky option but DON'T DESPAIR, you can still stop your food monster in his tracks. You need to teach him to sit on his bed while you cook. Take him to his bed, sit next to it with treats, say the word BED and hold the treat on the bed. The dog doesn't get the treat until all FOUR PAWS are on the bed. If he puts two feet on, that doesn't count – no treat. You'll need to repeat this several times. Once he's got the command, progress to standing in the kitchen and saying the word BED so he goes to the bed but don't KEEP giving him treats. Once he's got the word, that's it.

### Teach clear, consistent commands

Murphy's family were all using different commands so I also taught him (and them): UP, OFF, SIT and STAY so they had a handful of obedience commands to use which would stop him jumping up and stealing food off the surfaces or dining table. If you have a small dog who is jumping up at food, move your food right to the back out of reach and teach the command OFF. Simple as that.

### Don't feed your peckish dog from your plate

Never mind keeping your elbows off the table, dogs' table manners leave a LOT to be desired. We need to keep their noses away from our food. However sweet his little face is, NEVER feed your dog from the table or your plate. If your dog sits and stares at you, begging while you eat, you need to stop it. NOW. Lots of people are strict with their dogs through the week but then the Sunday roast rolls around and they're carving the chicken straight into the dog bowl. DON'T DO THIS!

To get your dog to stop begging at the table, teach him the STAY command. Do a mock-up dinner time to do this training, otherwise your food will go cold. Soggy spuds? NO THANKS! You'll have to keep leaving the table and taking him to his bed. Pop him on the bed and say STAY. Then make your way back to the dining table BACKWARDS so you're still facing him. That way he's still focused on you. Sit down and continue with your meal. He might creep back out and come to the table again. You'll need to repeat it over and over until he gets it.

### Don't make meal prep mistakes

When you're making meals or prepping food, don't drop little bits down on the floor for your dog. One for me, one for him. You know what I'm saying! If you add all those bits up on a plate, they would probably equal a human-sized portion of food. Keep your dog's food to his actual food.

### Limit his garden access

Most people's back doors to their gardens are in the kitchen so that's another reason that dogs often have unlimited access to the kitchen. We need to get rid of this mentality that dogs need access to the garden all the time. They DON'T. You wouldn't leave your toddler in the bathroom all day. You should have set routines for when your dog needs to go to the toilet. You let them out, they toilet, you bring them in and swiftly OUT of the kitchen again.

### Mix up meal times

Dogs and humans don't need to eat their meals at the same time. CRAZY IDEA, RIGHT? When you do this, you're creating a shared bonding environment over food and teaching your dog to eat with you. Dogs eat twice a day but we have three meals plus snacks. The maths isn't working, is it? So many people say, 'Oh I felt sorry for him so I gave him a bit of toast after breakfast' and then tell him off at dinner time, saying 'STOP BEGGING!' Those people have trained their dogs to beg!

### How's Murphy doing now?

Munchie Murphy is a reformed rogue. The sausages are safe! Sophie gets to eat her own birthday cake. All Murphy needed was a physical barrier and some clear commands. He'd stolen food for four years and was lucky he'd never been seriously ill from it. And his waistline looks better for sticking to the new raw diet!

'Ban your hungry hound from the kitchen. He's not Gordon Ramsay – there's no need for him to be in there!'

### 3 kitchen nightmare mistakes you might be making

**1. Feeding your kids near your dogs**
Small children regularly throw food on the floor or drop their snacks. Dogs aren't stupid and will patrol the bottom of the highchair looking for things your little one has dropped. BUT lots of those snacks, like raisins and grapes, are POISONOUS to dogs so keep your dog away while your children eat.

### 2. Not being consistent with boundaries

Allowing your dog a human treat now and again teaches him he's allowed your food. If you have a dog who steals food, don't give him human food AT ALL.

### 3. Storing food in easy-to-access places

Think about food in the same way as medicines and store it up high, out of reach. If you have things stored away for special occasions like chocolate eggs for Easter or fruit cake at Christmas (both poisonous to dogs), don't make the mistake of keeping them somewhere your doggy pal can find them.

### Leon's top tip

It's irrelevant WHEN you feed your dog – whether you feed him before you eat or after you eat, it doesn't matter. What matters is they have a CONSISTENT routine of feed times. That does NOT mean fixing their eating times with yours. It should, ideally, be separate.

## Get it right from the start: Food training for puppies

From frantic around food, to calm in the kitchen, here's how to nail it from the start.

1. Make sure that you don't go overboard with treat-based rewards when you're training your puppy. This can make him food OBSESSED. Once your dog has learned the command, he's learned it. At that point, STOP giving him treats.

2. Teach your puppy obedience commands right from the START. If he knows OFF and STAY then you'll be a long way towards keeping him away from your afternoon snacks or your Sunday dinner!

3. If it's not working, ask yourself WHY. You'll likely find that you're not being consistent or clear. Someone in the house will be using one command, and someone else will be using a different word and confusing the dog.

4. Prep your environment for your puppy, like when you bring a baby home. Make sure his bed is somewhere safe, keep him out of the kitchen, store food and medicines high up, out of reach. Set things up safely from the start and reassess regularly.

# CHAPTER 14

# SEPARATION ANXIETY

'My dog has gone from being a happy-go-lucky pup to stressed out with separation anxiety. We need a solution!'

Meet Bobby, the super-stressed dog with separation anxiety.

---

## Bobby's case file

**Dog's name:** *Bobby*
**Breed:** *Labrador*
**Age:** 7
**Sex:** *Male, neutered*
**Owners:** *Valerie, Richard and their daughter, Rose*

### Behavioural concerns?
• Separation anxiety – howling, frantic scratching at the door and carpet

### When did these behaviours start?
• Built up over three months with the breakdown of the family unit

---

---

**What food do you feed?**
- Raw diet

---

> 'Bobby was looking for his best friend,
> Rose, but she wasn't there!'

When Valerie and Richard separated, Richard moved out of the family home. In the back-and-forth between the two houses, Bobby became increasingly stressed with separation anxiety. Dogs rarely come into consideration when families break up but divorce also affects DOGS. The couple got Bobby as a puppy when their daughter, Rose, was little and they grew up together as best friends.

When Valerie decided to move out of town with Rose, leaving Bobby behind with Richard, Bobby lost the plot. He'd never been separated from Rose, his best friend, before. He was stressed and frantic. He'd follow Richard all around the house like his shadow and if Richard popped out to the car, he'd howl the house down. He was ripping up the carpet and clawing the doors even if Richard just went to the shop. He couldn't bear to be alone! Richard's neighbours were complaining and he knew he needed to sort Bobby out.

## THE POWER OF THREE: Bobby's assessment

### 1. Diet
Bobby was already on a great raw diet with Richard prepping his food for him. Brown rice, chopped up veg or sweet potato with chicken or salmon. Tick! Brown rice and sweet potato are both complex carbohydrates and have more nutritional value for your dog that regular carbs, helping add fibre to their diet. We didn't need to do anything there. He wasn't spoiled or over-indulged, just really taken care of. He'd been on this diet since he was a puppy so I knew his issue wasn't anything to do with his food.

## 2. Environment

Bobby's whole world came crashing down with the divorce. His day-to-day life was unrecognizable. He thought his best friend had ABANDONED him! Because of how quickly things deteriorated with Bobby's behaviour after the separation, I knew that it wasn't being caused by Richard leaving him for too long or anything like that. It was about Rose, his favourite human, disappearing from his life. We needed to address this. And fast!

## 3. Mental stimulation

Bobby had a great social life. The family had consistency with a dog walker and weekly doggy day care which both continued after the divorce.

---

### Bobby's 3-step stress-free separation solution

1. Carry on feeding a complete raw diet, twice a day.
2. Keep consistency in his life with doggy day care and regular walks.
3. Fill the void caused by Rose leaving him.

---

### How to smooth out separation anxiety stresses

Okay, let's get on with it and talk about how YOU can help your dog deal with separation anxiety.

### Fill the void

You can't explain divorce to a dog and I saw straight away that Bobby was pining for Rose, grieving for his best friend. I took Richard to a big toy store and we bought an oversized, floppy rag doll. YES, REALLY! We needed a toy that Bobby could carry in his mouth and put in his bed. And something that wouldn't be a choke risk. When choosing a toy like this, make sure it's something your dog won't destroy. Once we'd got the doll, I got a small ticking alarm clock and put it inside the rag doll so it mimicked a heartbeat. It wasn't that she looked like Rose – it was about having something with him that gave him comfort, like a child's security blanket.

## Make a date

I told Richard to cancel all his plans, stock his fridge and spend the weekend – 72 hours – with Bobby and the rag doll. We needed that three-day window with no separation triggers. Richard wasn't allowed to leave the house, not even to nip to the car. Poor Richard! I said, 'You're going to feel trapped but for the sake of Bobby's mental health, you need to do it.' It was important that Richard, the doll and the dog all bonded so Bobby could start to feel SAFE.

## Let your dog decide how and when to interact with the replacement

I told Richard that I didn't want him to pick up the doll or move it or anything, just prop it next to Bobby's bed and see what happened. Bobby was following Richard like a shadow but then he'd go back to check on the rag doll and forget to follow him for a moment. It was almost like his obsession started to shift from Richard to his doll. By the end of the weekend, Richard was able to go upstairs to have a shower without Bobby following him because the doll was doing what I'd hoped it would do, giving him *security*.

## Regulate your routine

If your dog has suddenly started suffering with separation anxiety, you need to look at what has changed in your routine. Have you moved house? Is your relationship breaking down or a new one starting up? Have you moved the dog's bed to another room? Have you changed your work patterns so your dog is on a different timetable now? Are you leaving them too long? Are they getting enough mental stimulation? Are they getting the right food? It might be something really small but it can feel really BIG to your pooch. Dogs love routine so try to keep it the same.

## Don't reinforce the chaos

All the 'traditional' dog-training books tell you to build up to leaving your dog alone. First, they say, wait outside the front door, then leave him for five minutes, then ten, then twenty and so on. ABSOLUTE NONSENSE! Dogs can't tell the time. There is no purpose in doing it in steps like that, you're just making a BIGGER thing of it. If you leave him, you should leave him for at least 45 minutes. If you're checking him after five minutes, he hasn't had time to settle down. The initial 'OH MY GOD WHERE HAVE THEY GONE?' is still going to be high so all you're doing is coming back while he's still stressed and frantic. You're rewarding stressed or unwanted behaviour rather than showing him that once he's calmed down you come back. You're reinforcing the chaos and negative association.

### Don't make a fuss on leaving or returning

Put down your white hankie, stifle the tears and save the farewell dramas. Seriously! People make *such* a big SONG AND DANCE when they leave their dog and when they come back in, 'Oh you clever boy, you've been so good while daddy's been away!' NO! WE DON'T NEED TO DO THAT. We walk in and we act NORMAL. Act as though you've just stepped out to pick the milk off the doorstep. You leaving has to become his new normal. And when you leave, don't hype him up and then disappear.

### Resist Radio Ga-Ga

People leave the radio or TV on when they go out but dogs don't need that sound stimulation. They might also hate that radio station or TV show! We think we're being nice – 'We'll leave it on because then he can hear something' – but because we might like that as humans, it DOESN'T mean it's right for our dogs. They need to be in their little bed, with a chew or nice toy, no harsh lighting, a nice calm environment. Recreate the environment of going to bed – relaxed and stress-free.

### How's Bobby doing now?

Bobby's separation anxiety is a thing of the past. He still has his rag doll who goes everywhere with him. And he gets regular visits with Rose every fortnight. She adopts the rag doll as well. The three of them hang around together and Rose bosses them all around. When Rose leaves, Bobby has his dolly so there's no void. CUTE.

'You can't explain divorce to a dog.'

## 3 stressful separation mistakes you might be making

There's a lot going on with the breakdown of a relationship and dogs rarely get a look in on custody arrangements but they're often BADLY affected by the collapse of the family unit.

### 1. Not including your dog in custody arrangements
Visitation rights need to include the dog – they suffer from grief and loss too, and should be kept with the family unit.

### 2. Messing up his routine
Keep your dog's routine as normal as possible. Feed and walk him at his usual times. And be consistent with boundaries and commands across households.

### 3. Leaving him too long
Never leave your dog for longer than three or four hours at a time. Leave him with a chew or toy. Make sure he has plenty of water.

## Leon's top tip

Dogs only have a 72-hour memory for their environment. They live in the present. Once Rose left, it was like a death. Dogs grieve and mourn but after three days, they're left with grief PLUS a horrible empty feeling but they don't know WHY. It's awful. Lots of people make the mistake of getting another dog to keep them company but they'd still be grieving the first dog. The best thing to do is ENRICH their lives in another way to fill the void. This could be something

new like hydrotherapy or agility that they've never done before.
Or a new toy or dolly. Over time the grief will dissolve.

## Get it right from the start: Separation training for puppies

Be prepared from the moment your puppy sets foot in your home so he feels
comfortable and safe from day one.

1. Get a soft toy – you can get one that mimics a heartbeat, or just wrap
   a clock in a towel. The bottom line is you've just taken your puppy
   away from his mum and his brothers and sisters. He's traumatized.
   He needs comfort and reassurance. Being clingy is normal but it can
   easily become separation anxiety.

2. If you do crate training, 'traditional' training will advise you to leave
   him and not go to him when he's crying. It's brutal. Follow your gut and
   comfort him if he needs it.

3. A good breeder will ask you to bring a toy when you visit, which picks up
   the smells of the litter for you to take home with your puppy. Alternately
   they might give you a scrap of fabric from their bedding to bring home
   with him. This makes him feel less like he's been abandoned. It's a
   connection between the two worlds – old and new.

# CHAPTER 15

# FUSSY EATING

'My dog eats normally for three or four days and then goes off her food. We've tried EVERYTHING but nothing seems to hold her appetite for longer than a few days. And then we're back to square one.'

Bella the Welsh Terrier's demanding dinner times are causing her owners the same stress levels as silver service in a Michelin-starred restaurant.

## Bella's case file

**Dog's name:** Bella
**Breed:** Welsh Terrier
**Age:** 3
**Sex:** Female, spayed
**Owners:** Sarah and Timothy

### Behavioural concerns?
- Eats food one day and not the next

### When did these behaviours start?
- Puppy

**Previous training?**
- Three different trainers, none had worked

**What food do you feed?**
- We've tried everything!

'Dogs are driven by food and fun.'

Bella was a picky eater. She would go two days without eating and Sarah, her owner, would be having a mental breakdown thinking Bella was going to die of starvation. My first reaction was WHAT THE HELL IS GOING ON? It was like Gordon Ramsay's Kitchen Nightmare. Sarah and Timothy were doing everything that they SHOULDN'T do because they were so worried. In a panic, Sarah and Timothy would try a different food type and Bella would eat that for a bit, and then go off it, and the cycle continued. One trainer had even told Sarah to get on ALL FOURS like a dog at meal times next to Bella and eat her own dinner off the dinner plate on the floor because she didn't understand how to eat properly. AND SARAH DID IT!! At least she didn't have her eating actual dog food. Another trainer told them to hand-feed her! It sounds MAD but 99 per cent of training books tell you to hand-feed a fussy eater. You do NOT hand-feed a dog. Bella had these two running around accommodating her every whim.

## THE POWER OF THREE: Bella's assessment

### 1. Diet

Bella thought she was in a Michelin-starred restaurant, going through the whole menu. Garçon! She had her owners wrapped around her little finger. They would put a bit of tuna on the kibble and she'd eat it, brilliant. She'd eat that for three days, then on day four, she'd turn her nose up. Sarah would panic and swap the tuna for cheese, and Bella would eat that for a few days, and then stop. They had tried steak, chicken fillets, turkey, cod, pork, lamb, steamed vegetables, boiled vegetables, seasoning, no seasoning, petit pois, garden peas, mangetout, fresh joints of meat. Everything! BONKERS!

## 2. Environment

Bella was a very spoilt dog. She was QUEEN of the house, sleeping in the bedroom with the owners, probably on her own four-poster bed with memory foam mattress and flatscreen TV. The kitchen, where she was fed, was calm and serene like an interiors magazine so no complaints there. It's worth noting that dogs *can* be anxious about their feeding environment. If you're putting her food down next to the washing machine when it's on, that might stop her eating. You need to make sure you're feeding her in a calm, safe space away from machinery, noises, stress and people coming and going. And keep other dogs or pets away in case they snatch her food.

## 3. Mental stimulation

Bella went to doggy day care twice a week and was exercised regularly. She SHOULD have been hungry. Sarah had even taken her to the vets three or four times to get her checked out and there was nothing wrong with her.

---

### Bella's 3-step fuss-free food plan

1. Swap the demanding diva diet for a new complete raw food, twice a day.
2. Provide structure – not fuss – around meal times.
3. Take the ten-minute test.

---

### How to fix your fussy eater for good

Right, if you've got a diva dog like Bella, how can YOU train her to gobble up the good stuff as soon as it's put in front of her?

### Remember that your doggy diva won't starve

The first thing to know is that your dog WON'T starve herself. Some dogs can go five days – or even longer – without eating. Dogs are natural scavengers. They will eat whatever they want to eat and if they are hungry, they WILL eat. It's impossible for a dog to starve himself. IMPOSSIBLE. Their DNA and survival instinct kick in. The idea of a fussy-eating dog is UTTER NONSENSE. There's no such thing. I understand how stressful it is when your dog won't eat. But Bella was three years old, they'd tried everything, and she needed to be fixed.

### Check for injuries

If your dog is in pain or uncomfortable, that could be a reason they're not eating so like Sarah and Timothy, it's always worth getting your dog checked out first by a vet. If dogs have neck issues, spinal damage or limited mobility, feeding them from a raised bowl can help.

### You decide what's for dinner – not her

We moved Bella on to a raw diet of chicken, turkey or fish. Sarah said they'd tried raw before but had found it too bloody and were worried that Bella was going to die of salmonella. But I told them to try it. I suggested a really good complete raw food and I told them that they had to STICK to this new diet and not supplement it with bits of cheese or tuna or petits pois or whatever Madame Bella decided she'd eat that day. They were doing the equivalent of giving her a menu every meal time for her to choose from. NO. There's not a choice of 18 different options with starters, mains and desserts. TOUGH. Don't change her diet, don't add to it, just keep it exactly the same, meal in, meal out.

### Don't give your dog five-star fuss

Diners in a fancy restaurant expect high levels of service and fuss. Your dog does not. I told Timothy, 'She's like this because you make a big fuss over every meal.' They were hovering over her, watching and waiting, on hand with the parsley to sprinkle over her bowl if she wanted it. Take it down a notch. Let it be known that the food is there, walk away, supervise out of the corner of your

**MAX**
Bad recall

**JASPER**
Aggressive to visitors; biting

**ALFIE**
Fear of loud noises; barking at everything

## BETTY
Dancing on the dining room table; ignoring her owner

## TRIXIE
Aggressive to owner

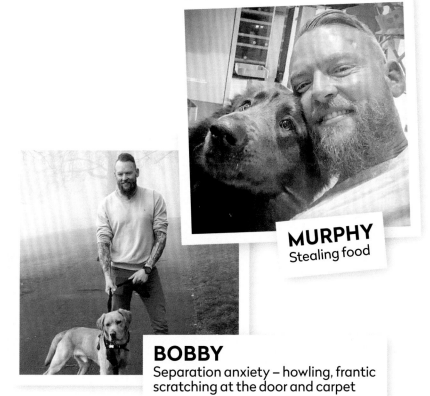

**MURPHY**
Stealing food

**BOBBY**
Separation anxiety – howling, frantic scratching at the door and carpet

**BELLA**
Eats food one day and not the next

**RIO**
Wees and poops in the house

**JAGO**
Pulling on the lead

**TEDDY & ROCCO**
Completely unruly – chewing,
digging, destroying and wrecking

## REX
Aggression to other dogs on the lead. Told he was untrainable and could never be with other dogs by rehoming charity; never mixed with other dogs

## LUNA
Eating poop – her own and other dogs'

**CHARLIE**
Constant whining

**LOTTIE**
Resource guarding of toys; snarling to lunging within four months

**ELLIE**
Excessive humping of furniture, soft toys and people

**BODHI**
Excessive licking of paws
and owner's hands

**ROSIE**
Growling and biting on the sofa

## RUPERT
Jumping on other dogs and pinning them to the ground

## TOBY
Lunging at cars, bikes and runners

eye at the other end of the room. Do not make a big deal. Do not hand-feed her. Do not say, 'Oh what's this, come and get your dinner' while tapping on the bowl.

### Take the ten-minute test

The owners were actually creating this situation because they left Bella's food down all day so that she could come and go. Leaving food down all day for her to graze takes away her DRIVE for food. Dogs are driven by food and fun. Like me! Sarah and Timothy had spent a lot on allergy tests and I said, 'The only test you need to pass is the ten-minute test!' It won't cost you anything. You put the food down, say your buzzword – DINNER – she has ten minutes to eat it. You don't make a fuss about it, and if she doesn't eat it within TEN MINUTES, you lift it and she loses that meal. You DON'T give her double at the next meal. We needed Bella's natural survival instinct to kick in, for her to see her food and think, 'I need to eat that now because if I don't it will be gone.'

### Hold your nerve

I understand the temptation to give in and add a little something to make her eat. DON'T. If she doesn't eat for two days, she doesn't eat for two days, she's not going to die. Her meal doesn't get replaced by a higher value food. You have to break the habit. On the third day, Bella ate. I've done this with other dogs and it's taken longer. They still have fresh water. I had a lot of phone calls, text messages, panic attacks and tears but they had to hold firm. It is new and it is *stressful*. I knew Bella was going to eat but her owners had to trust me. I said, 'I'm sorry but if you can get someone to tell you to get on all fours and eat your food like a dog, I'm sure you can trust me to tell you to leave that food and lift it after ten minutes. I'm not asking you to do anything ridiculous.'

### De-stress dinner times

Sarah and Timothy had tried loads of different bowls for Bella. They'd tried a metal bowl and said they didn't think she liked the sound of it, a ceramic bowl, a plastic bowl, a dinner plate, a human bowl, a pan, a frying pan, a raised bowl, a bowl with water attached. They did everything but set her a place at the dining table! Some dogs don't like metal bowls. If your dog wears a collar, their little pendent can clank against it. We settled on using a child's plastic plate with a tea towel on the floor so it didn't move around. You can get a slip mat to go under the bowl if you prefer.

## Lose the treats

People say, 'My dog isn't eating her food.' But they're stuffing her full of treats between meal times. Treats can fill her up. If you have a fussy eater, remove treats entirely until you've nailed meal times. If she's hungry enough to eat a treat, she's hungry enough to eat her dinner.

## How's Bella doing now?

Bella wolfs her food down within seconds. It was never a problem again. It's the same with all the dogs I've treated like this. They all turn out the same. They become that dog that eats their food as soon as you put it down. Some of them take it to the other extreme and we have to get bowls that slow down their eating because they gulp it down so fast!

'Dogs are driven by food and fun. Like me!'

## 3 feeding mistakes you might be making

### 1. Feeding your dog too rich a diet

Avoid game – duck, venison and pheasant – for dogs, it's too rich. I would never feed my dog game either as their main food or in treats.

### 2. Taking food from your dog

NEVER take food from a dog when it's eating out of a dog bowl. People are taught that they need to do that to prevent food aggression. There is NO purpose whatsoever in snatching food from a dog while they're in the middle of eating their dinner. Would you ever snatch your child's food away while they're eating? OF COURSE NOT. Loads of training books recommend taking food off your dog. NOT THIS ONE.

### 3. Not spotting an allergy

A lot of dogs are allergic to poultry. She would still eat but she would either be sick or have profuse diarrhoea every meal time. If that's the case, remove that food and try something totally different. If you're three food types down the line – for example, poultry, fish and beef – and your dog is still being sick, take her to the vet.

### Leon's top tip

Remember that dogs do NOT have the same tastebuds as humans. The average human is born with around 10,000 tastebuds whereas dogs have around 1,700. Dogs can identify sweet, sour, salty and bitter but they don't crave variety in the same way we do. They go off texture rather than taste. Owners always say, 'Oh they'll get bored of that.' They won't. They can have the same food all their lives. They understand high value food like cheese and roast chicken because of the SMELL.

### Get it right from the start: Fuss-free feeding for puppies

Make sure you don't encourage your puppy to be a fusspot around food by following these tips.

1. Decide what your puppy will eat and stick to it. Don't chop and change her food around. It can upset her stomach.
2. Don't make a fuss of feed times. Pick a consistent buzzword that you'll say when you put food down – DINNER or DIN-DINS – and then leave her to it.
3. Don't encourage your puppy to graze by leaving her food down all day. She should always have water but take her food up after ten minutes if she hasn't eaten it.

## How to slow down greedy guzzlers

Some dogs have the opposite problem to Bella and wolf their food down. Rescue animals are a classic example of this. What can you do if your dog is inhaling her meals?

1. Make sure your dog is wormed and doesn't have parasites that could be causing her to gobble her food. And make sure her food is nutritious enough.
2. Feed her on her own. Some dogs bolt their food if there are other animals around, so make sure the environment is calm for her.
3. Use a slow-feeding bowl so she physically has to slow down while she eats. There are loads of different options so you can find the right one for you and your dog.

# CHAPTER 16

# TOILETING TROUBLE

'My dog wees and poops all over the house even though he's five years old. How do we save our carpet and our sanity?'

Meet Rio, the Great Dane with a great big poop problem.

## Rio's case file

**Dog's name:** Rio
**Breed:** Great Dane
**Age:** 5
**Sex:** Male, neutered
**Owner:** Tilly

### Behavioural concerns?
- Wees and poops in the house

### When did these behaviours start?
- Puppy

**Previous training?**
* Nothing

**What food do you feed?**
* Dry kibble 3 times per day
* Rawhide treats

## 'If your dog poops or pees in the house, you have to get rid of the smell COMPLETELY.'

Rio, the Great Dane, was keeping his owner Tilly on her toes with his constant toileting in the house. And being the size he was, these were no dinky poops. These were like elephant poos! He was pooping in the living room, squatting in front of her while she was watching *Bake Off* and parking a chocolate log on the floor! SURPRISE SHOWSTOPPER! He was also peeing on everything. Tilly came home one day and it looked like someone had spilled chocolate milkshake all over the bed but Rio had diarrhoea caused by Tilly giving him three rawhide chews in quick succession. He would *occasionally* toilet on walks but it was hit and miss. Tilly would walk him round the block and he didn't do anything and as soon as they got home, he toileted.

And when Rio was toileting, it was a really stressful environment. Tilly thought that Rio was doing it in the house out of spite, saying, 'But he poops right in front of me and looks at me while he does it. He does it on purpose.' She was shouting at him. I drew the line there. Dogs don't have an emotion called spite. They don't hold grudges. They don't try to get revenge. Get that out of your head right now. Rio isn't the protagonist in a Jackie Collins novel. He's a DOG.

## THE POWER OF THREE: Rio's assessment

### 1. Diet

Rio was being fed too much food, too late at night – about 8.30pm – which would cause a dog to need to toilet overnight anyway. Tilly thought that by feeding him later he wouldn't need to go to the toilet until morning. I asked, 'How's that working out for you?!' NOT SO WELL. He was on a diet of kibble, three times per day like a puppy. Because he was a big dog, she thought he needed constant feeding so she just kept filling his bowl up and she had no idea how much he was actually eating. All that dry kibble and rawhide treats gave him the biggest thirst. Things like pigs' ears and rawhide are pure animal fat. It's like eating two big bags of pork scratchings. You'd be GASPING! Your mouth would be hanging out!

### 2. Environment

Rio had the run of the house so he was able to toilet EVERYWHERE. Cocking his leg on the curtains, pooping on the bed. People think the bigger the dog, the more space they need to roam around. They don't. The kitchen was PLENTY big enough for him. A dog should be able to lie down fully, stretch out, stand up and do a full 360-degree turn for a room to be big enough. Tilly kept the back door to the garden open all day. Keeping the door open doesn't teach your dog HOW to go to the toilet. When Rio went to the toilet in the house, Tilly wasn't cleaning it up properly. She'd scoop it up, spray some carpet cleaner down and give it a rub. And that was it. In her eyes, she'd got rid of it. But Rio could obviously still smell pee and poop, which tells him this is where I'm meant to pee and poop.

### 3. Mental stimulation

Rio was getting walked properly and going on play dates to the local park with quite a few dogs. He was socially active and exercised so no problems there.

---

### Rio's 3-step poop plan

1. Forget the fatty diet and swap it for a healthier complete raw food, twice (not three times) a day.
2. Restrict his access around the house with a tall safety gate.
3. Set up a Rio Routine for his meal and toileting times.

---

## How to fix your toileting terror

Let's talk about how YOU can house train your dog and avoid messy mistakes.

### Swap the salt and forget the fat

Before we did anything else, we needed to get rid of Rio's salt-laden, fat-heavy food. I put Rio onto a strict, healthy raw diet – chicken, turkey, fish – and moved him to two feeds per day. He was getting loads of rawhide treats which, because they're fatty, were causing more bowel movements and a really bad smell. We stopped those too. The salt content in his diet was making him drink gallons, which meant he was always dying for a wee. Raw food doesn't have all the salts and yeast that his dry food had. The DIFFERENCE we made just by changing his food was *unbelievable*!

### House train your dog

I asked Tilly to tell me what kind of house training she'd tried with Rio. And I was met with a blank look. She had kept the back door open for him and assumed that when he needed to go to the toilet, he would take himself outside to do it. Er, NO! Not if you haven't TAUGHT him that's where he should go to the toilet. She had just assumed that dogs understand the difference between indoors and outdoors. THEY DON'T. But she expected Rio to just KNOW!

### Learn your hound's habits

You should always know your own dog's toileting habits from a health perspective but especially if you're toilet training. If you're a good owner you know when he goes to the toilet, how many times per day, how much is normal or not normal, consistency, smell – the works. If you don't know, you need to PAY MORE ATTENTION.

## Go back to basics

I told Tilly to take a week off work. It's like having a puppy again. She needed to teach Rio what she should have taught him when he was a puppy. She needed to give him her full attention, watching for any signs that he needed the toilet. She had to be vigilant. If he'd been asleep, she had to take him out when he woke up. After he'd eaten or had any water, she had to take him outside. I told her that she needed to pick a word to encourage him to toilet – QUICK, TOILET, WEE-WEE, POO-POO, whatever. It didn't matter WHAT the word was but it needed to be *consistent*.

## Let's go outside

Dogs can't differentiate between indoors or outdoors. You have to teach them. If you wanted to train your dog to wee or poo on a spot next to the fireplace, you could do it. Quite the party trick! You have to teach him to toilet outside. After that first toilet of the morning in the garden, set an alarm for every hour and take him outside to toilet. I knew Rio wouldn't relieve himself every hour but by doing this, Tilly was able to learn his toileting habits.

## Praise at the RIGHT time

Don't make the mistake of saying GOOD BOY half way through his wee or poop because he'll nip it, get all excited, and come inside and then half an hour later, do the rest on your carpet. Don't say ANYTHING until he's finished. As soon as he's finished and he goes to walk off, give him LOTS of praise. Verbal praise only. Don't use treats. There's no need.

## Remember that accidents happen

If your dog does pee or poop in the house, do NOT tell them off. If you find a wee or poop in the house, don't say, 'Who did this?' and tell them off. NEVER wipe your dog's nose in wee or poop. It's cruelty. I want to make that VERY clear. We positively reinforce the good behaviour (toileting outside) and ignore the unwanted behaviour (toileting inside). People don't realize that when the dog has started toileting, you have to just let them do it. People grab their puppy and shriek and carry them outside. Stopping them mid-flow can cause urinary tract infections and your dog won't understand why you tell him off one time and not the next. It can also cause anxiety and confusion. If he's already mid-flow, ignore it and clean it up.

### Make those floors sparkle

If your dog poops or pees in the house, you have to get rid of the smell COMPLETELY. Say hello to your clean-up crew. YOU! The only way to eradicate the pong of poop and the whiff of wee from your home is by using white vinegar and warm water. Call me a domestic goddess if you want (please) but it's the only thing that works and it doesn't cost a fortune! This stops habitual toileting. A lot of cleaning fluids have ammonia in them, which makes dogs think that's where they should toilet.

### Watch the water

You wouldn't give a toddler a pint of water to go to bed with because they'd wee the bed but Rio's water was down on the floor ALL the time. That's not great if your dog has an issue with toileting. Once we'd sorted Rio's diet and I knew exactly what he was getting, I could safely tell Tilly to lift his water at 8pm and replace it the next morning. Taking water away from a kibble-eating dog would be cruel but dogs on a raw diet drink a lot less water. Tilly had to leave it down all day but overnight, I didn't want Rio tanking up. This will depend on the temperature. If it's summer or a warm day, leave your dog's water down. I told Tilly to monitor how much he drank because it would be *much* less when he wasn't on salty kibble and fatty chews. Once his toilet training was complete, we went back to giving him total access to water at ALL times.

## Rio's new routine

We changed Rio's feeding times dramatically by making a routine with set meal times and set toileting times.

6–7am: Wake up and take him to the toilet in the garden
7–8am: Breakfast
Mid-morning: Walkies
Lunch time: Garden for toileting
Mid-afternoon: Walkies
4–5pm: Dinner
5–9pm: Toilet in the garden

## How's Rio doing now?

It took Rio ten days to get the hang of things but it could take another dog a month or longer. We don't expect toddlers to pick up potty training in a week so why do we expect that from dogs? Five years of toileting all over the house. Sorted. I told Tilly to treat herself to a whole new carpet! God knows, she needed it!

'We don't expect toddlers to pick up potty training in a week so why do we expect that from dogs?'

## 3 ways you might be causing poop problems

### 1. Feeding too late
You should feed your dog NO LATER than 5pm if you're going to bed at 10–11pm. Any later and you run the risk of him needing to poop in the night.

### 2. Not knowing your dog's routine

You should know when your dog needs to go to the toilet and make sure he's able to go when he needs to. Having a routine – for feeding, walking, toileting – will make this much easier.

### 3. Not cleaning up properly

If your dog toilets in the house, make sure you thoroughly clean the mess up, otherwise he'll be able to smell it and think that's where he's supposed to go to the toilet.

### Leon's top tip

Avoid overuse of puppy pads. The only time I'd use them is overnight. Leave one down while your puppy is learning to be dry through the night. If you're crate training, chances are their crate will be dry anyway because dogs don't like to toilet in their own environment. It's a LAST RESORT to mess their own crate. Don't put a puppy pad in the crate – it's ridiculous! Using pads all the time means you're training your dog to toilet inside the house. It doesn't make sense. Training them on puppy pads for two weeks until they get used to toilet training means double the work. They're a waste of time and money.

### Get it right from the start: House training for puppies

Remember, a puppy's bladder is the size of a teaspoon and they don't have the muscles to hold in their wee or poop until they're much older. But here's how to encourage them to toilet outside and not on your favourite rug.

1. Don't feed your puppy too late at night. Dogs shouldn't be fed any later than 5pm if you normally go to bed 10–11pm. By bringing their

evening meal forward you can make toilet training happen a lot quicker.

2.  Take your puppy out every hour during waking times but not overnight. Don't get up in the night with them – that's training them to get up in the night to toilet. If they eat early, you can be confident that they won't need to poop in the middle of the night.

3.  Establish a feeding and toileting routine that works for your household – and stick to it.

## 'My dog has suddenly started weeing in the house what do I do?'

1.  If your normally house-trained dog starts toileting in the house and it's not an age thing, I'd take them immediately to the vet for a check-up as that would indicate a bladder infection.

2.  It could also be stress-related if his environment has changed – if you've got a lot of shouting in the house, separation, someone leaves or someone new moves in, these things can be factors.

3.  People randomly change their dog's food and that can affect their toileting – look at their diet and don't forget the treats he gets.

# CHAPTER 17

# PULLING ON THE LEAD

'My dog is so strong on the lead that he pulled me over and broke my nose. He's a danger to himself and others.'

Meet Jago, the Rhodesian Ridgeback, who is always in a rush.

---

## Jago's case file

**Dog's name:** Jago
**Breed:** Rhodesian Ridgeback
**Age:** 3
**Sex:** Male, neutered
**Owner:** Marie

**Behavioural concerns?**
- Pulling on the lead

**When did these behaviours start?**
- Puppy

---

**Previous training?**
• Three behaviourists and trainers – most did treat-based training

**What food do you feed?**
• Dry kibble

> 'Marie had broken her nose when Jago pulled her over so she'd stopped walking him for her own safety!'

Joyful Jago was fine OFF the lead and had great recall but ON the lead, he was a nightmare – mega-excited, dragging his tiny owner Marie along in his wake. It was like he was permanently racing his own shadow with 5ft Marie trotting along trying to keep up. Marie had broken her nose when Jago had pulled her into the bushes and she fell flat on her face. He was so excited to get to wherever they were going that he ploughed ahead as fast as he could without thinking about Marie.

He'd pulled on the lead since he was a puppy but as he'd got bigger, more muscly and stronger, it was like being dragged around by a HORSE. She'd tried three other trainers, who had all suggested treat-based training where you stop and give the dog a treat and then set off again. All that does is teach the dog to pull, then get a treat and then pull again. This method hadn't worked and she was thinking she'd never be able to walk him again, which was understandably upsetting her. She'd been given the wrong advice and she didn't know what to do.

## THE POWER OF THREE: Jago's assessment

### 1. Diet
Jago was over-energized from an excess of carbs. Carbs convert to sugar, which is why Jago was like Tigger on a diet of energy drinks! BOING!

BOING! His dog food was one of the most expensive on the market, one that vets encourage you to buy, but it had NO meat content in whatsoever, which was shocking! Always check the meat content of your dog's food. It was all animal derivatives and the rest was carbs. It had them all: brown rice, white rice, potato – any carb you can think of was in that expensive food. This issue would never have been resolved just with training because the diet was a MAJOR part of the problem.

## 2. Environment

Marie had a large garden and that's where she was letting Jago exercise several times a day. She was responsibly trying to keep both herself and Jago safe by not walking him. If I'd felt there was any issue with his welfare, I would have stepped in but there wasn't.

## 3. Mental stimulation

Although Marie was avoiding walking Jago on the lead, he came to us for doggy day care twice a week so he was getting more exercise than other dogs who were being walked seven days a week, tearing around with all his pals and getting masses of mental stimulation.

---

### Jago's 3-step learner-on-a-lead plan

1. Reduce this racer's sugar intake to lower his Tigger-like energy by introducing a raw fish diet (he had an allergy to white meat) before we could begin lead training.
2. Make sure Marie has the right gear – try the 'triangle' or Halti.
3. Rewire the owner-dog remote control to learn how to walk safely.

---

### How to fix your dangerously dragging dog

If your dog pulls like a runaway train on the lead, what can YOU do to rein him in and keep everyone safe?

### Try the triangle method

Marie had tried using a collar and lead and a harness so I introduced her to a different option, which you might have seen on *Embarrassing Pets*. It's called THE TRIANGLE. It's a split lead where one bit attaches to the collar and the other attaches to a harness. We tried this first so that we weren't pulling on Jago's neck at all. This is really important! People fail to realize that if you have a lead or collar on your dog that is strangling him, he will try to ESCAPE that sensation, which means he will PULL even more. He doesn't understand it's the collar and lead causing the pain so he will just try to run away, making the problem a million times worse.

### Introduce the Halti hero

Marie didn't like the triangle method, so we tried Jago on a Halti. These are like headcollars for dogs and they're brilliant. They're safe and they actually make the dog feel more secure. We took two weeks to slowly introduce Jago to the Halti. I introduced this the same way I introduce muzzle training (see Chapter 5). I told Marie that this was the most important part. Once she'd got Jago used to the Halti without him feeling trapped and trying to rip it off, then she'd done the hard work. Once he was happy with the Halti, we practised walking round the garden. Then we walked round the corner to the park. I handed her the lead and she said, 'Oh no, I'm scared.' I reassured her that if anything happened, I was on hand to grab him. Marie walked Jago to the park, he had a run around, and Marie walked him home. SUCCESS!

### Rewire your remote control

We needed to stick 'Learner' plates on both Jago and Marie and go right back to basics. I told Marie to think of Jago's lead as a REMOTE CONTROL. It was her way of communicating to him and telling him what she wanted him to do, as well as a way for her to get information from him. I told her that *she* was in control of the lead, not him.

### Walk the walk

HOW you walk your dog is key. So many people get this wrong. This isn't about being the 'leader' and the dog being behind you. It's not that stupid Pack

Theory stuff! It's about enjoying a RELAXING walk with your dog. When you walk your dog on the lead, the arm attached to the lead should be in line with your leg, relaxed, down by your side. It shouldn't be in front, behind, or out to the side. People are so used to walking their dogs with their arms out in front like ZOMBIES being pulled along that people think that's how you *should* walk them. It's not. If you have a big dog like Jago, he's going to pull your shoulder out because he weighs 48kg (106lb). No one needs that! Your dog should never pass the front of your feet. He should be by your SIDE. His head should be facing forwards and not trailing on the floor like an old pair of curtains, walking with meaning and purpose.

### Hold him in one hand

People are commonly told to hold the lead in two hands – holding the lead in their left hand and the loose part in their right with the dog always on your left side. Don't do this! If you fall or trip, like Marie, and you have the lead in both hands like she did, you'll break your wrist or your nose because you'll go flat on your face. Instead, hold the lead in one hand, down by your side, loose. And don't wrap the lead around and around your hand – if your dog pulls, you'll break your fingers.

### Follow the inside track

For safety reasons, your dog should always be on the INSIDE and NEVER next to the road. You wouldn't walk your toddler right next to a road, you'd put yourself between them and the traffic. Hold the lead in whichever hand you need to use to keep him on the inside.

### Stick to a short lead

Keep your dog on a short lead, not a long lead or – God forbid – an extendable lead. I BLOODY HATE THOSE THINGS! They are SO DANGEROUS. I had a client who used one with her Cocker Spaniel and the wire wrapped round her finger and took the top of her finger off. She was left with just bone! And they're dangerous to dogs. What do you think happens when a dog goes racing off? It has to come to a stop at some point. HELLO WHIPLASH! Keeping your dog on a short lead next to roads is VITAL. Just because your dog has never run off or been bothered by traffic doesn't mean he won't be scared and leap out in front of a lorry. I have seen it happen.

## Reluctant walkers

### No sniffing matter

You don't want a dog trailing behind you on a walk, dragging him up the road like old Eeyore, because he's sniffing every blade of grass. Yes, it's important for dogs to sniff but if you're going round the block to the park, I'd argue that they can do their sniffing AT the park. I would encourage them not to keep stopping but keep them moving forwards. People say, 'You're not letting him have any freedom.' It's like taking your children to the park. When you get to the park, that's the fun stuff, but on the way there you have to think SAFETY. You are not being cruel to ask your dog to walk beside you.

### Get him checked out

There's no reason why a dog wouldn't want to go outside for a walk so ALWAYS get him checked by the vet because he might be in pain. You might think he's being a stubborn old mule but he might have arthritis or sore paws and need treatment.

### Turn him around

If your dog IS simply being stubborn and wants to go a different route to you, turn him around and walk the other way, then reverse it and go back the original way again, and then switch it again and say COME ON in a bright, encouraging voice and walk with purpose. Keep doing this until he's moving happily forwards. DON'T wheedle, 'It's okay, don't be scared' because that feeds into their anxiety and you're creating more of an issue than there was in the first place.

## How's Jago doing now?

Jago is a reformed boy racer. I was so proud of Marie because she had felt like such a failure before and was carrying this constant guilt that she wasn't walking him every day. She burst into tears when we made it out onto the lane for the first time. I told her, 'You did that! You did the hard work.' She didn't give up, even after three other trainers and a broken nose!

'Think of your dog's lead as a remote control,
a way for you both to communicate with each other!'

### 3 on-the-lead mistakes you might be making

#### 1. You must be choking
I am REALLY against choke chains, half choke chains and slip leads used as a lead. These pieces of equipment are STRANGLING your dog. People say that dogs have different neck muscles. They don't. These collars can still harm them. I would only ever use a slip lead if I was doing a figure of eight, where you have it over the dog's nose and around the back of the head. It doesn't touch the neck at all.

#### 2. Letting him jump up
Smaller dogs get away with this, launching themselves at other people with their muddy little paws. If your dog does this when you're walking, you need to teach him UP and OFF (we cover command training in Chapter 4).

#### 3. Trying treat-based training
I wouldn't use treat-based training for pulling on the lead. You don't want to teach your dog that the more he pulls, the more treats he gets, and the faster he gets somewhere.

## Leon's top tip

Really think about the commands you're giving your dog on the lead. My pet peeve is HEEL. What EXACTLY do you want your dog to do when you say HEEL? People say 'HEEL! He's not listening!' I would either say WAIT or COME ON. Ask yourself, have you actually taught him what you want him to do when you say that word? He doesn't just automatically know what HEEL means. You have to teach it. Dogs ALWAYS want to please. So, if he's not doing it, there's been a breakdown of communication somewhere and it's usually the OWNER!

### Flat-nosed dogs

Brachycephalic dogs, or dogs with short or flat noses like bulldogs, pugs, French bulldogs, Boston terriers and boxers, can't wear Haltis. If you can't put a Halti on your dog, I would use the triangle method. If your dog has had spinal injuries or a neck injury, then I would use a harness and NOTHING else.

### Get it right from the start: Lead training for puppies

It's important to walk your puppy OFF the lead when they're young to help with your recall (see Chapter 8). But to make sure your dog enjoys walking ON the lead, you need to train them.

1. Start by walking him round the garden on his lead and do his toilet training on the lead while he's waiting for his vaccinations. People don't think to do this until you take him out of the house for the first time. If you leave it too late, he'll be terrified and won't understand why you're pulling his neck.
2. Once he's had all his jabs, you can introduce him to all the new smells and sights of the great outdoors on the lead!
3. Make sure you don't encourage your dog to bite and play with the lead by making it into a game.

# CHAPTER 18

# DEMOLITION DOGS

'Our dogs have destroyed our homes, dug up the gardens, ripped the sofas and shredded the curtains. We don't know what to do!'

Meet Teddy and Rocco, the double-trouble brothers with a destructive wild side.

## Teddy and Rocco's case file

**Dogs' names:** Teddy and Rocco
**Breed:** Black Labradors
**Age:** 7 months
**Sex:** Male, not neutered
**Owners:** Brothers Oliver and James

### Behavioural concerns?
- Completely unruly
- Chewing
- Digging
- Destroying and wrecking

**When did these behaviours start?**
- Puppy

**Previous training?**
- None

**What food do you feed?**
- Dry kibble
- Treats – chews, pigs' ears, gravy bones

'It was like a puppy playground. The curtains were like grass skirts, still hanging up but totally shredded. The gardens were wrecked.'

Teddy and Rocco were Labrador puppies and litter brothers. Their owners were two brothers, Oliver and James, who lived next door to each other. The dogs were completely unruly – and had been from day one. When I arrived, Rocco was jumping on Oliver's head, bouncing along the back of the sofa, while Teddy attacked the sofa cushions, which were held together with duct tape! It was like a puppy playground. The curtains were like grass skirts, still hanging up but totally shredded. The gardens were wrecked, just potholes where they'd dug down like they were trying to find Australia, mud flying behind them all over the windows. I said, 'I don't know how you can live with this! I've been here half an hour and my head feels like it's going to explode.' Oliver and James sat on the sofa and said, 'It's easier for us to sit still and let them get on with it. They'll have a mad hour and then it's fine.' But it wasn't fine. It was NEVER fine. It was a mad 24 HOURS every single day. People put up with the maddest things from their dogs. A 26kg (57lb) dog wrapped around your neck like a SCARF?! Sure! They were out of their depth, not even trying to stop them. They asked if I wanted a cup of tea. Never mind a cuppa, I need a Valium!

## THE POWER OF THREE: Teddy and Rocco's assessment

### 1. Diet

The puppies were eating LOADS of carbs. The brothers were giving them four Weetabix (cereal wheat biscuits) each with cow's milk for breakfast because the breeder had recommended them. Honestly! They were having about ten packets of digestive biscuits a day as well. They thought it was fine because they weren't the chocolate ones, 'We know you can't give them chocolate before you say anything!' It's more the fact you're giving them ten packets of biscuits love! They should have had shares in McVitie's! They had cornflakes for supper. Jean said, 'It calms them down!' DOES IT REALLY? Never mind that there's no nutritional value for the dogs. Then they were chucking kibble in whenever. It was ludicrous, like giving kids a bag of fizzy sweets every meal time. The dogs would counter surf and jump on the counter tops whenever they wanted snacks. Bear in mind these puppies weren't dainty little tea-cup-sized dogs. They were 26kg (57lb) by this point. Big stocky Labs.

### 2. Environment

Both houses were TRASHED. There were no dog beds because they'd shredded them. The sofa looked like a teabag, it had that many holes in it! These two big puppies were just running and jumping, bouncing off the walls and onto the bookcase which displayed the Disney ornaments Oliver collected. It was like a tornado had gone through Disneyland! The tail was missing off Pluto and the ears gone off Mickey Mouse. Jean pulled out a spongy neck brace and said, 'I have to wear this on an evening because if I'm not careful they'll pull my neck. I've already done it twice.' OH MY GOD! I couldn't believe what I was seeing! There was no routine to waking, feeding, walking. NOTHING. The dogs could hear each other through the walls of the houses so they'd howl and bark at 5am, deciding what they were going to trash that day. They were like a puppy version of the bloody Kray twins!

## 3. Mental stimulation

The only mental stimulation these dogs got was mentally torturing their owners. They had such high energy levels and there were TWO of them! Like Dennis the Menace and Minnie the Minx, egging each other on, shredding things, fighting in the middle of the living room. They weren't being walked, just flung out into the garden to dig and destroy.

---

### Teddy and Rocco's 3-step boisterous boys' plan

1. Chuck out the cereal and carb-heavy food and get these pups onto a healthy raw diet to help them grow and develop without filling them full of sugar.
2. Start doggy day care and limit their access around the house with safety gates.
3. Firmly establish boundaries in these chaotic households. These boisterous boys needed routines and rules.

---

## How to fix your destructive dog's damaging ways

Right, let's discuss how YOU can stop your dog's demolition derby.

### Read the riot act

Oliver and James needed to know that this behaviour was NOT acceptable under ANY circumstances and it was down to THEM to change it. They'd never had dogs before and had bought these boys on a whim, but it was time to GET SERIOUS.

### Chuck out the cereal

The cereal HAD TO GO! I wanted to get their diet completely clean so I moved them both onto a raw chicken complete food. No more human cereals. They said, 'Oh they're not going to be happy.' And I replied, 'I don't care. You're the parent, they're the child.' Just by reducing the carbs I predicted that in the next 3–7 days they would see the puppies' energy levels decrease by half. I also explained that once they were on the raw diet, we didn't give them treats like gravy bones because that would spike their energy again. Twice a week they would have raw chicken wings with a raw egg cracked over their food, including the shell, to help clean everything out, like a detox. Take a look at Chapter 3 for more information on this.

### Structure meal times

Because they were puppies, they needed three meals per day. I recommended their new meal times were 7am, noon and 4pm. I wanted them to do this for two weeks before I came back to start training. It wouldn't have been fair on the dogs to try to train them while they were still amped up on carbs.

### Start doggy day care

These dogs were FULL of energy and testosterone and desperate for mental stimulation so I told the brothers to research 'dog day care near me' during those initial two weeks while the dogs were on their new diet. I wanted the boys to have already had their first day care assessment by the time we began training.

After their first day in day care, they didn't move! That was the FIRST time the brothers had had any peace and quiet. It worked magically as I knew it would. When a dog goes to day care twice a week, the benefit spreads across the whole week. I never recommend consecutive days because it's too much so the boys went on Mondays and Wednesdays to break the week up. Those two days fulfilled their mental stimulation need for the entire week.

### Keep them separate

I explained to Oliver and James that the dogs shouldn't be together all day, they needed to keep them separate for certain periods. Dogs from the same litter can have Litter Syndrome where they don't listen to humans or respond to human interaction. They have each other, in their insular little world, a bit like human twins can have their own language. It can make them really hard to train.

### Create a safe space

I saw that the boys needed their own individual safe spaces and time apart in the evening, like their own little bedroom, so we did crate training. We did it on the days they'd been to day care so they were more tired and less bouncy and gave them each a cosy crate in their respective kitchens. You can read more about crate training in Chapter 5. A lot of people buy crates that are far too big for their dogs. A dog should be able to stand up, do a complete 360-degree turn and lie down sprawled out fully. We were able to put bedding into the crate without them destroying it because they'd been to day care and their energy levels had reduced due to their new diets. If we'd done that before it would have come out shredded to sawdust.

### Impose house rules

Once we had one dog per house, we started to impose a bit of order. We put safety gates up to limit access to the kitchen. They had been jumping on the washing machine and dryer, and walking along the worktops like baby elephants, helping themselves to whatever food they fancied.

### Get them off the sofa

We needed to teach them some commands to stop them jumping up and using the sofa as a race track. We cover all eight commands I teach in Chapter 4. We did UP and OFF with Teddy and Rocco. I wanted the brothers to tell the dogs to get OFF the sofa if they jumped up. The dogs should only be on the sofa if they've been *invited* UP. We supplemented these commands with SIT. To teach a dog to SIT is a natural movement for dogs. If done properly the dog's head follows your hand moving upwards and naturally their bottom touches the floor as they go backwards. It's a bit of a trick really. Get your dog in front of you and purse your fingers together and raise your hand up and say SIT.

### Stop the digging and destruction

We needed to teach these diggers to down tools. We did this with the commands LEAVE and GO. The hand sign for LEAVE is to make an 'L' of your thumb and first finger, like the sign for 'Loser'. Put it in front of your face and then move it out away from you with an outstretched arm, have a treat in your other hand and get the dog to focus on the treat. Bring the treat towards the 'L' hand and then outstretch your 'L' hand saying LEAVE, LEAVE. They will associate the hand movement with the treat. Then put the treat on the floor but keep eye contact the whole time. They will naturally take their eyes off the treat and look at the 'L'. Say LEAVE in a firm but fair tone. Leave a large pause and then repeat it once to keep them focused on your hand. Then you can teach him GO. The signal for GO is the thumb and forefinger of your previous 'L' held on its side to point like an arrow. And then they can take the treat. Once they've understood the command, they get no more treats. This works for digging in the garden or any kind of destructive behaviour.

### Just say NO

The boys responded to the new commands so well. They loved that someone was FINALLY in charge. Dogs are followers. People talk about pack leaders and top dogs (we cover this in Chapter 2). NO. It's not true. Dogs like to be led. That's why a parent-child relationship works so well. We needed to add two more commands into the mix – WAIT and NO. WAIT is a flat hand raised. Same routine as with LEAVE. Put your treat in your other hand. Put your arm out in front of you. WAIT – WAIT. Then GO is the release again.

And the word NO. This was an important one for these delinquents. To teach NO, turn your 'L' towards them, pointing at them, and say NO. Nine times out of ten, they'll look at you and start doing what they were doing very slowly while still looking at you as if to say I'm still going to do it. Pause. Then say NO again firmly with eye contact.

### Structure their play

If you have a destructive dog, don't leave their toys out because they'll destroy them. This kind of destruction is boredom based. If they're bored of the toys, that tells you they shouldn't be there all the time. We didn't want to schedule play time right before bed time because it would wind them up right when we wanted them to be calming down. We structured solo play times to mid-morning and mid-afternoon, where all the toys came out; we let them go crazy for half an hour, then put them away where they couldn't see them. The boys needed separate play times because they played together at day care twice a week and the brothers walked them together each day as a joint activity.

## Keep your boundaries

You have to be *consistent* with boundaries. Weekends have to be the same as week days. Everyone in the house needs to stick to the rules. The brothers really stuck to their guns but their wives kept slipping the dogs biscuits and being really negative.

## How are Teddy and Rocco doing now?

I went back four weeks later for a follow up. I went to each house separately and then I got them to meet up and saw them together. They were like different dogs because the brothers had put the work in. It was the humans that had needed training! The funny thing was that because the dogs calmed down, the brothers realized their respective partners were really annoying and negative and they had got rid of them!

> 'Dogs like to be led. That's why a parent-child relationship works so well.'

## 3 destructive dog mistakes you might be making

### 1. Bribing your dog
You can't reward a dog for doing something you don't want him to do. He'll just think you want him to do it even more.

### 2. Ignoring their behaviour
Ignoring destructive behaviour won't make it go away so you need to teach your dog what is and isn't acceptable in the house.

**3. Giving them free run of the house and car**

A dog that has access to the whole house or who is left alone in a car can do a LOT of damage. Limit his access with safety gates in the house and dog grills in the car, and don't leave him alone in the car.

## Leon's top tip

Dogs love chewing. As well as play time, we also have chew time at day care. An hour in the morning and an hour in the afternoon. Don't leave the chew lying around, give it to him for an hour at a time.

## Get it right from the start:
## Dealing with destructive puppies

When a puppy chews, there's a misconception in the dog world that they do it because they're teething. Puppies chew because they're BORED. It's a lack of mental stimulation and we're reading it so wrong.

1.  Take them to puppy socialization parties and to the park. Puppies need stimulation so get them out every morning to socialize. Put a little post on Facebook asking if there are local people to do a meet up. Day care might be too much for them all day but we take puppies from 14 weeks old for half days.
2.  Puppies need to chew. Give them something natural to chew – yak milk chew, olive branch, coffee branch – so they're less likely to go for your table leg.
3.  Don't divert. If your puppy is busy dismantling the sofa, don't give him a treat or pet him. You're telling him, good boy, well done, I really liked

it when you put a hole in the sofa. Instead use the word NO or LEAVE. And be firm but fair.

4. When dogs ARE teething, you'll find their teeth on the floor, like little shards of glass. You could freeze a carrot or get an old rag and knot and wet it, then freeze it. That feels really good on their gums.

# CHAPTER 19

# FEAR AGGRESSION ON THE LEAD

'My dog is aggressive to other dogs, going crazy, barking and lunging. We'd love to be able to let him socialize with his peers. Help!'

Meet Rex, the rehomed Romanian rescue dog with anger issues.

## Rex's case file

**Dog's name:** Rex
**Breed:** Romanian rescue dog
**Age:** 2
**Sex:** Male, neutered
**Owners:** Abbie and Chris

### Behavioural concerns?
• Aggression to other dogs on the lead
• Told he was untrainable and could never be with other dogs by rehoming charity
• Never mixed with other dogs

**When did these behaviours start?**
- Prior to them rehoming him - they got him aged 6 months

**Previous training?**
- Five other trainers, none had helped

**What food do you feed?**
- Dry kibble

'Abbie and Chris had spoken to five other trainers who hadn't been able to help. They had fobbed them off saying, "He'll never be able to mix with other dogs."'

Rex's anger issues towards other dogs were so bad that he was going to be euthanized! If he saw another dog walk past within 100m (328ft), he would go crazy and sound like he was going to kill them. He couldn't cope with his feelings at all. His owners, Abbie and Chris, got him through a Romanian rescue charity where he'd been since he was tiny. He'd been picked up off the street and had been badly abused by humans. He was scared and didn't even know how to play. This was a dog with deep psychological issues that he'd had since he was a puppy. Abbie and Chris had spoken to five other trainers who hadn't been able to help. They had fobbed them off saying, 'He'll never be able to mix with other dogs.' They didn't give him a chance. Abbie and Chris didn't know where to turn. They were exercising him when it was dark to try to avoid other dogs. Going out early in the morning, last thing at night, anywhere they could go to avoid seeing another dog. It was too stressful for them and for him.

## THE POWER OF THREE: Rex's assessment

### 1. Diet

Rex was on kibble, full of carbohydrates and only 9 per cent meat. The rest was animal derivatives, brown rice, white rice, potato, all the usual stuff. The carbs were turning to sugar which was fuelling his anxiety and fear aggression. I moved him onto raw chicken for working dogs – 85 per cent chicken and ground bone, 15 per cent vegetables, minerals and nutrients.

### 2. Environment

His home environment was fine. Around the house Rex was the perfect gent. But when he saw other dogs, the red mist descended. He was like JEKYLL AND HYDE. They'd take him in the car to the middle of nowhere to walk around, sniff and exercise, or walk him late at night in the dark. Guess what? That's when everyone else with an aggressive dog is out. It's the worst time to go. It's a TOTAL bloodbath.

### 3. Mental stimulation

Rex had NEVER EVER mixed with other dogs because of his behaviour. I knew straight away that it wasn't dominance aggression or outright aggression. This was FEAR AGGRESSION. Rex was TERRIFIED of other dogs. When a dog is on the lead and kicks off at another dog, as humans we think, 'Oh my God that dog is vicious it's going to kill my dog.' It's actually the complete opposite. A silent dog – a silent assassin – is much more dangerous. It's the quiet ones you need to watch, not the ones barking and kicking off.

### Rex's 3-step fear-facing plan

1. Devote time to the Drip-feed Technique (see below) to help turn a negative trigger into a positive experience.
2. Socialize safely with bomb-proof dogs.
3. Don't expect an overnight miracle – keep up regular, consistent training.

## How to fix your fear aggressive dog

I'd say 60 per cent of dogs are reactive on the lead. It's a HUGE problem and owners get really embarrassed about it. But it's really common and YOU can fix it. Here's how.

### Fight the fear

If a dog is fearful and they feel trapped, they have a FIGHT OR FLIGHT response. If they're on the lead, they physically can't get away so they think they have to FIGHT, which is why those dogs react more on the lead. It's a much more common problem than people think and owners can feel isolated by their 'failure' but it's often the result of bad advice. People say to walk your dog in the dark or hide behind a parked car if you see another dog. But that's not dealing with the situation, it's avoiding it so it goes unfixed.

### Remember size doesn't matter

Dogs don't differentiate by size, which is why you'll get a Great Dane trying to sit on your knee. Dogs see energy levels and movement. Your dog might be aggressive to another dog not because he's bigger, but because he moves differently to your dog or he has higher energy levels.

### Fix the problem

The 'typical' approach to this issue is to use food – a treat-based, scatter feed tactic. When you see another dog, chuck a load of treats on the floor and get your dog to divert their attention. But we know that diversion tactics DON'T FIX THE PROBLEM. I prefer to face problems head on. I have my own unique training method to help dogs with fear aggression on the lead. I call it the DRIP-FEED TECHNIQUE. When a dog licks, it helps relax and soothe him. We used this natural behaviour to help Rex with other dogs. Using a block of Brussels pâté, we helped turn Rex's NEGATIVE trigger – other dogs – into a POSITIVE experience. For this to work, your dog must lick the pâté straight from the tub. Don't let him *eat* it, he has to LICK. It's not about shovelling food in. You might need to freeze it.

### Befriend some bomb-proof dogs

We needed a selection of bomb-proof dogs who were completely confident and settled and who wouldn't be messed up by our controlled exposure to Rex. We also needed a large, safe space where Rex could SEE another dog but not be anywhere near him. We used the field at our day care centre but you can book local dog fields for these kinds of training sessions. We had Rex on the lead at one end of the field, and one of our bomb-proof dogs on a lead at the other end, 100m (328ft) away.

### Make eye contact

I wanted Rex to SEE the other dog. I wanted the visual NEGATIVE trigger to be taken away by using the POSITIVE licking experience of the pâté. The other dog needed to be far enough away so Rex could start licking the pâté before the red mist descended. I stood with Rex, getting him to lick the pâté, while Dean, my partner, had the bomb-proof dog at the other end of the field. We had walkie-talkies so once Rex was licking the pâté, I said, 'Right bring the dog onto the field now.' Rex HAD to make eye contact with the other dog. I wanted him to see and watch the other dog while he was licking the pâté. Don't block his view – that's avoidance.

### Let him lick

With the Drip-feed Technique, the dog needs to be licking the WHOLE time. As soon as Rex stopped licking, we STOPPED. Dean would slowly move forward with the bomb-proof dog a few strides and stop. Rex continued to watch them and LICK-LICK-LICK. And the bomb-proof dog kept progressing slowly towards him.

### Provide a positive experience

I could tell the exact moment the trigger became too much for Rex because he stopped licking. At this stage, even three strides in a session was amazing progress for Rex because of the severity of his issue. But we waited until Rex started licking again when he felt comfortable, and we moved a bit closer again. We moved three strides each time; while Rex was licking, we kept progressing. All this time we were changing Rex's thought process. We were taking the negative trigger, which was visual, and creating A POSITIVE EXPERIENCE by licking the pâté. Subconsciously his brain was already changing. Abbie and Chris couldn't believe that we'd got another dog within 50m (164ft) of Rex without him kicking off.

### Socialize safely

I knew from that first session in the field that I wanted to try him in our day care. Abbie and Chris were terrified, thinking he'd attack another dog, but I just knew in my gut he would be fine. Because he had fear aggression, we could get the right blend of dogs and help him socialize. It's safer to have a dog in our day care with 30 other dogs than it is to let your dog off the lead with five dogs in the park. You don't know what those other dogs are like, whereas the dogs in our day care have all had behavioural assessments. We organized a short ten-minute 'meet and greet' session with four other bomb-proof dogs. We didn't want to overwhelm him and make it into a negative experience. LET'S NOT UNDO ALL THE GOOD WORK. Meeting other dogs off the lead would increase his confidence, create independence, give him social skills and teach him how to speak dog. Dogs learn from each other without human interference. Rex had never had that before.

### Make sure your safety catch is on

In this case, Rex's safety catch was a muzzle. Before we could get him into the day care, we needed him to be muzzle trained (see Chapter 5 for more detail on this). The muzzle would keep him and the other dogs safe. People don't like putting muzzles on their dogs because they think other people will see them as dangerous. But if Rex had nipped somebody, even if it wasn't his fault, because of his previous behaviour he would have been blamed.

### Pick your mix well

On D-Day – Day care Day – we did a training session first to tire Rex out. Then we popped his muzzle on. We had four dogs in that morning and I was confident they would be a good mix for Rex. I took him in and the owners stayed outside because if he'd got over-protective over them, or he'd picked up on their nerves, it could all go wrong. Abbie and Chris had NEVER seen him interact with another dog so we took some video to show them.

I let Rex off the lead wearing his muzzle and he ran away barking. One of the other dogs went up to him and he went mad. Barking and snapping. He wanted to play but he was giving the wrong signals. He thought he was initiating play but the other dogs read it as aggression. He was like the gobby person at the pub, 'Come on, I'll have you.' But he settled and we were eventually able to take his muzzle off! It was lovely. I had a little cry. For Rex to get close enough to another dog to sniff them, lick them, touch them was like, BLOODY HELL, his life has just been enriched massively. It was beautiful. Abbie called me SOBBING down the phone when I sent her the video.

### Don't expect an overnight fix

Even though Rex was fine in the day care for ten minutes, we hadn't cured his extreme on-the-lead fear aggression. I told Abbie and Chris to pause training and bring him into day care, half a day, twice a week for six weeks. He built up slowly to meet more dogs until he was happy with 15–20 other dogs, building his confidence up – a key part of reducing his fear aggression.

### Take small steps

After six weeks of day care, we did the field exercise again with the Drip-feed Technique using different dogs. It went really well and we got Rex within 10m (32ft) of the other dog before he reacted. That's MASSIVE. Some people might say, 'He's still barking' but this was a dog who would LOSE THE

PLOT if another dog was 100m (328ft) away and now he's okay with one being 10m (32ft) away.

## Separate exercise from training

Your training should be completely separate from exercise, don't get the two mixed up. And don't try to do the two together. You should walk your dog for exercise and then do ten minutes of your training program EVERY DAY. Do just 10–15 minutes per day – no longer because you don't want to set your dog up to fail or have them get bored. I asked Abbie and Chris to find four or five non-reactive bomb-proof dogs. It was important that they didn't bark because he would have gone crazy. They could be friends' dogs or they could find them by putting a post on Facebook asking for non-reactive dogs on the lead for a training exercise. I wanted them to do a structured exercise, using a different dog each day in order to train him to be okay with all dogs. They had to sit somewhere like a bench and give Rex his pâté to lick and have the other dog walk past.

## Practise every day

When they'd done it with those dogs enough times, they could progress to dogs they didn't know. They needed to practise for 5–10 minutes every day somewhere quiet with no dogs off the lead or kids running around screaming. The last thing we want is a dog off the lead running over or a to-do with a toddler. You want dogs going past but not too close, almost like a coffee shop environment.

## How's Rex doing now?

This was an EXTREME case so training is still ongoing but Rex is already SO much better than he was. Not every problem is going to disappear overnight. Abbie and Chris can take him out wearing a muzzle to keep him safe. They can walk round the park now and see other dogs on leads but I would still not let him off the lead in an uncontrolled environment outside of day care. He's learned how to speak dog and he's learned how to play normally. He's doing amazingly at day care, where he can interact with any group or dog, no issues. I'm confident that he'll be able to walk with other dogs on the lead in time. But it will take time. He'd never interacted with another dog and eight months later he can mix with 20 dogs and interact and socialize completely naturally. AMAZING.

'Rex has learned how to speak dog!'

## 3 fear aggression mistakes you might be making

### 1. Overwhelming your dog
If your dog has fear aggression, you need to introduce other dogs slowly and safely. Don't be tempted to throw him into the deep end. It will backfire!

### 2. Diverting attention
Lots of people will turn around and walk the other way if they see another dog or try to put themselves or an object (like a car) between their dog and the other dog to block them. This isn't dealing with the problem. Some experts recommend scattering treats on the ground to distract your dog from the other dog but it's AVOIDANCE and what happens if you don't have treats with you one day?

### 3. Shouting at your dog
Screaming at your dog while he is barking will escalate the situation. Instead, ignore the behaviour. If he's reached the red mist, there's no return.

**Leon's top tip**

You can tell your dog is fear aggressive if he lunges, barks, snaps, growls, spins on the lead or snarls at other dogs. That immediately tells me that's FEAR because a truly aggressive dog would be SILENT. There'd be no warning, he could even be wagging his tail. 'Oh, he's wagging his tail, he wants to say hello.' No, he's about to rip your dog's head off. When the dog's tail is up like a poker, flickering fast like a rattle snake, WATCH OUT.

## Get it right from the start:
## Anti-aggression training for puppies

No matter what size your puppy is, they should be trained not to show aggression to other dogs.

1. Socialize your puppy properly with other dogs. Introduce him to as many friendly dogs of different shapes and sizes as possible. Do this on the lead as well as off the lead.

2. Don't pick your dog up when he's barking. People think, 'My dog's smaller, he's going to get eaten' and they pick them up. By cuddling him when he's in the red mist, you're encouraging the heightened aggressive behaviour. You're basically saying, 'Well done, I love it when you do that.' Instead, leave him on the ground on the lead.

3. Don't neuter your puppy too early – this can cause a massive loss of confidence as their natural stores of testosterone or oestrogen disappear. We cover this in detail in Chapter 5.

# CHAPTER 20

# POOP EATING

'My dog eats poop. It's disgusting! She's not fussy – she'll eat her own or other dogs' mess. How can we get her to stop?'

Meet cute little Luna, the cockapoo with a stomach-churning diet.

## Luna's case file

**Dog's name:** Luna
**Breed:** Cockapoo
**Age:** 5
**Sex:** Female, spayed
**Owners:** Jim and Nicola

### Behavioural concerns?
• Eating poop – her own and other dogs'

### When did these behaviours start?
• They noticed it at a family party but it had likely started before then

**Previous training?**
- No

**What food do you feed?**
- Dry kibble

'There's no such thing as a poo fairy!
Luna's been hoovering it up love.'

Whenever Jim and Nicola let Luna out into the garden for the loo, Luna would eat the poo that hadn't been picked up from the night before. She also ate other dogs' poo on walks. Jim and Nicola only realized that Luna was a poop eater during a barbecue in the summer. They had friends over with their two dogs and Luna was running off and coming back looking very pleased with herself. Their friend suddenly screamed out, 'Oh my God, Luna's eating her own poo!' PASS THE SICK BUCKET. A lightbulb went off over Nicola's head, 'I wondered why I could never find poo to pick up when I went round the garden!' Where did she think it went? THERE'S NO SUCH THING AS A POO FAIRY NICOLA! Luna's been HOOVERING it up love.

### THE POWER OF THREE: Luna's assessment

### 1. Diet

Luna's kibble only had 4 per cent meat. It was overloaded with salt, yeast and preservatives. Any dog that eats its own or another dog's poo does it because they're lacking nutrients in their diet. It's the only reason a dog would eat another dog's poo or their own. Even if it's habit, the habit would have started as a result of a poor diet. Because of what they're lacking, the poo smells appealing to them. Dogs understand the different values of food by the smell of them. Luna saw any other dog's poo as a high-value treat.

## 2. Environment

If you're leaving dog poop around the garden, you're giving your dog opportunities to eat poop. Always make sure that when your dog toilets, you pick up straight away, even last thing at night. If you don't, you run the risk of her going out first thing, being hungry and scoffing down whatever she deposited the night before.

## 3. Mental stimulation

Luna had a busy social life and would always run up to the other dogs, for obvious reasons, seeing what they had! 'What have you got in your packed lunch?' Unfortunately, while she was socializing, she was also scooping up poop. It had become a habit, which we needed to break.

---

### Luna's 3-step poop-eating plan

1. Get Luna onto a complete raw diet to give her body the food and nutrients she'd been craving.
2. Reduce Luna's opportunities to scoff down the stinky seconds.
3. Invest in muzzle training until the habit is fully broken.

---

## How to fix your dog's dirty appetite

It's unpleasant but someone's got to deal with it. Let's find a pain-free process for YOU to teach your dog to give up the poo eating.

## Fix the diet

In order to address the problem head on, we needed to change Luna's diet. We had to replace her nutrient-deficient kibble with something cleaner and packed full of goodness – a raw chicken complete diet full of vitamins and minerals. This gave Luna everything her body needed and had been craving.

### Check if it's a learned behaviour

Occasionally an owner will say they've changed the dog's diet but the poop eating has continued. That's because it's become a learned behaviour. It's disgusting to us, but Luna was being rewarded in her eyes every time she ate poop with a delicious 'treat'. She was getting nutrition from the waste of the other dogs who were on better diets. This tasty 'treat' was reinforcing the unwanted behaviour.

### Break the habit

Although we changed Luna's diet, the poop eating had become a habit, so while we waited for the diet to kick in (2–4 weeks is normally enough) she needed to wear a muzzle when she was off the lead so she couldn't eat anything while she was out of Nicola's sight. See Chapter 5 for details on how to do this.

### Clean up your mess

No, the poo fairy does not exist. HATE TO BURST YOUR BUBBLE! Dogs can be quite secretive about poop eating so a big sign is if you can never find dog poo to pick up in your garden. It certainly isn't biodegrading overnight! Watch your dog carefully when she goes out to toilet so you can see what she's up to. And as soon as she poops, you need to swoop in with a bag and CLEAN. IT.UP.QUICK.

### It's not naughty

Let's bust the myth that dogs eat poop to be 'naughty'. It's seen as 'bad behaviour' and something they've always done and can't be stopped. People say this rather than looking at the problem and asking why a dog does it. What is causing your dog to do it? There is always a reason. But it's never because they're naughty.

### How's Luna doing now?

Luna's one-woman waste disposal business is now out of action. She's abandoned her addiction to poop eating. With a cleaner, healthier diet, she was getting everything she needed from her food so she no longer had to forage for poop and Jim and Nicola weren't giving her the opportunity by keeping their garden clear of mess.

'Luna's one-woman waste disposal
business is now out of action.'

## 3 mistakes that could be causing your poop-eating problem

### 1. Not picking up
The number one way to stop your dog eating poop is to limit her opportunities to do it. Pick up any poop straight away. Don't wait.

### 2. Feeding a poor diet
Giving your dog food that lacks nutrients and real meat will make her more likely to try to find what she's lacking elsewhere. Where? You guessed it – other dogs' poop!

### 3. Reinforcing the habit
By not addressing the problem straight away, you will reinforce the habit, making it harder to kick. Every time she eats poop, she sees it as a TREAT or reward. Only restricting her access to poop – both in your garden and out on walks via a muzzle – will break the habit.

## Leon's top tip

Don't let your dog kiss you on the mouth. As Luna proves, dogs aren't always the most hygienic creatures where their mouths are concerned. Stomach churningly, Nicola had been letting Luna kiss her lips – something she quickly stopped, I can tell you!

## Get it right from the start:
## Avoid your puppy becoming a poop eater

Making sure we get things right from the start can prevent our puppies from becoming obsessed with eating other dogs' poop.

1.  Feed your puppy an appropriate diet, rich in vitamins and minerals, from the start. Don't wait until there's a problem to fix.
2.  When you're toilet-training your dog, make sure you pick up and dispose of all waste STRAIGHT AWAY, not in an hour, not in the morning. IMMEDIATELY. Puppies are inquisitive, don't give her the opportunity.
3.  Don't punish your dog for poop eating if you catch her doing it. Instead, work through the steps above to make sure it doesn't become a habit.

# CHAPTER 21

# ATTENTION SEEKING

'My dog whines constantly for attention. We play games with him, take him for walks, do puzzles, make sure he's fed. But he never stops! What can we do?'

It's always whine o'clock with Charlie, the attention-seeking Staffy-cross.

## Charlie's case file

**Dog's name:** Charlie
**Breed:** Staffy-cross
**Age:** 9
**Sex:** Male, neutered
**Owners:** Maureen and Fred

### Behavioural concerns?
• Constant whining

### When did these behaviours start?
• Since forever

**Previous training?**
- They'd had a behaviourist who had tried avoidance techniques using treats

**How often is Charlie walked?**
- Twice a day for two hours each time

**What food do you feed?**
- Dry kibble and tinned meat (not good quality, with animal derivatives)

'Their whole lives – day and night – revolved around entertaining this dog.'

Charlie's owners, Maureen and Fred, were retired but they probably had LESS to do when they worked full time. Charlie had become their boss. Their whole lives – day and night – revolved around entertaining this dog. He'd have his toy game and get bored of that after ten minutes and Maureen would be shouting, 'Get his licky mat Fred!' Ten minutes later, he needed something else. If Maureen sat down, Charlie would put his head on her knee and whine, a very annoying, high-pitched noise. It got right under your skin and it was NON-STOP. They'd seen a behaviourist who had told them, 'If he's whining, chuck him a treat or a toy.' Well, HELLO BAD ADVICE! You're rewarding his unwanted behaviour! Maureen said, 'It works while he has the treat and then he starts again.' I BET HE DOES!

## THE POWER OF THREE: Charlie's assessment

### 1. Diet

Charlie's diet was poor. It was the equivalent of an ADHD kid not getting their medication. You're chucking fuel on the fire. We changed his food to a raw fish diet because he had an allergy to poultry.

### 2. Environment

Bless these two but they DOTED on Charlie and *literally* spoiled him rotten. Everything they did revolved around that dog. They had all the time in the world and they showered Charlie with love and affection to the point where they had ruined him. He had toys everywhere. It was like the toy aisle of PETS AT HOME. His wish was their command.

### 3. Mental stimulation

Fred walked Charlie for two hours each morning, and two hours each afternoon, but he didn't have proper structured mental stimulation. They chucked a constant barrage of stuff at him – toys, treat games, a licky mat. They were doing everything they were told to do but he needed structure.

---

### Charlie's 3-step whine o'clock plan

1. The key part of this is the training of the owner, yes YOU! We have to train *you* to ignore your pup's plaintive pleas.
2. Make time for mental stimulation, no matter what age your dog is.
3. Schedule time for rest – it's as important as play!

---

### How to fix your annoying attention seeker

Whether you've got an older dog like Charlie who you don't think can learn new tricks, or your dog has just started whining, let's see how YOU can get some peace and quiet from your pet.

### Dive into day care

We got Charlie into day care for two half days a week. Full days would have been too much for him at his age and being so used to being at home with Maureen and Fred. We built it up from an hour the first time to a half day. It knackered him out for the whole day because it was PURE mental stimulation. It worked so well that Maureen and Fred were worried and called the vet and the day care. 'He's not right Leon, he's not spoken to us all night,' they told me. They were worried about his health and I was like, 'Never mind HIS health, he's going to put the pair of YOU into an early grave!'

### Remove your attention

If you have a bored dog, any attention you give him, even negative attention – 'Be quiet! Shut up!' – is still *attention* and therefore a reward. Some trainers say to ignore the whining and then when he stops praise him. But tell me, why would it be a good idea ten minutes after they've stopped crying to say, 'Oh Good Boy, well done, you've stopped whining'? Because GUESS WHAT? He's going to start whining again! You're going to get the full repertoire of every song he knows! In Charlie's case, it's become a learned behaviour because he's done it for nine years.

### Temper your tone of voice

People don't realize the effect of their tone of voice. Owners often think that the dog can understand everything they say to them. I'm not saying it's not lovely to sit and talk to your dog. I used to do it with Scooby all the time (he'd walk off into another room and I'd think, 'God even he can't be bothered with me!'). But if every time your dog whinges and whines, you say, 'Shush you're fine, you're going to get your dinner in ten minutes' in a sing-song voice, he thinks you're saying, 'What a lovely little song you're singing, thank you, do you know any more?' You're encouraging it.

### Ignore it

Most owners have a lack of awareness at how often they are pandering to their dog's attention seeking. Everybody does it. But to put an end to attention seeking and crying, you have to COMPLETELY IGNORE HIM when he's whining. It should be as if he's not there. Don't even make eye contact. It is SO hard. Owners say, 'I didn't say anything to him' but they were looking at him. That's still acknowledging him. It's like cold turkey FOR THE OWNER. Maureen and Fred had fed this habit for nine years! It was like a dripping tap. They needed to learn a new behaviour as well as the dog. When his chin is on your knee and he's looking up at you with puppy dog eyes, it's VERY HARD. But you MUST ignore him.

### Structure his play time

Maureen and Fred were retired so they had all the time in the world to work out a schedule for Charlie. Rather than having millions of toys and his licky mat and puzzle games and everything else out ALL THE TIME, I asked them to structure in two play times per day, one in the morning, one in the afternoon. This is when Charlie's toys would come out and they would actively play with him. At the end, they'd tidy the toys away until next time.

### Make time to rest

Let your dog rest! Poor Charlie was set up to expect CONSTANT attention from Maureen and Fred. Instead of hurling a barrage of activities and toys at your dog, plan your day so that he has his walk, his meals, his play and his mental stimulation, but he also has time to REST. Get your feet up, Charlie, and relax! He's been out for TWO HOURS. He'll need a sleep. You don't need to constantly give your dog attention – it's unnecessary and your dog ends up wound up because he *needs* down time.

### Be realistic

Old dogs can learn new tricks but this kind of habitual behaviour isn't just going to stop overnight because we've changed his food and started him in day care. He's done this for nine years. We need to have realistic expectations. He's not going to become a silent dog who lies on his bed overnight straight away, but if you stick with the training, it will happen.

## Get through the first 72 hours

Dogs live in the here and now. Anecdotally, from my experience with tens of thousands of dogs over a decade, I believe that dogs have a 72-hour memory. Dogs have triggers rather than memories. When they see you after your two-week holiday, they fill up with endorphins caused by a positive trigger. And when people say their dog was initially excited to see them and then sulked for a few days, that's because their trigger (your face) didn't match your smell. You've been using sun cream and eating different food so you smell different. As that wears off, they stop 'sulking' because you match again.

Equally, a negative trigger tells them they're in danger. That might be a person who looks like someone who abused them or a dog that looks similar to one who attacked them. But it's not a memory. If you're teaching your dog something new and trying to get rid of a learned behaviour it will become easier after 72 hours, even if you don't feel like you're progressing at all. After 72 hours they seem to reprogram and reset, no matter what age the dog. His new routine will start to become embedded. But those first 72 hours are VERY hard.

## How's Charlie doing now?

Once Maureen and Fred were trained, Charlie was much better. Don't get me wrong, they went through HELL trying to ignore little Charlie's pleas. They were on the phone to me every single day, texting me saying it's not working. I told them to bear with it and keep going. I had warned them that the first 72 hours would be awful. They were ignoring him and he was still whining. 'WHY ISN'T IT WORKING?!?' It's not a case of ignoring him for an hour, you have to be consistent. With lots of encouragement they held firm and now Charlie lets them put their feet up without singing them his latest tunes.

### 'Old dogs can learn new tricks!'

## 3 moaning mistakes you might be making

### 1. Making eye contact
You might have fought the urge to say anything to your whining Whippet, but if you're still looking at him when he's crying, it's attention. Act as though he's not there.

### 2. Giving up too quick
The first 72 hours are the WORST. Get past those and you'll crack it, I promise. But so many people cave before that. I've had people tell me that they've ignored him for an hour and it hasn't worked! You've got to give it time.

### 3. Overstimulating your dog
If your dog is set up to expect constant attention and play time then he'll cry to remind you if you 'forget'. Make sure you schedule in plenty of DOWN TIME in your dog's day.

## Leon's top tip

Create a timetable for your dog: wake up, breakfast, mid-morning, lunch time, mid-afternoon, dinner, bed time. In each box write what you will be doing – that DOESN'T mean there should be an 'activity' in each box. You should look at that planner and see a pattern of REST, whatever age your dog is. If you don't then you're doing too much. There has to be the same amount of rest as there does mental stimulation and play time. Having your dog's routine somewhere visible means everyone in the house will stick to it.

## Get it right from the start:
## Attention-seeking training for puppies

When you get a new puppy, you want to do the right thing so you read all the books, research online, go to the pet shop and you end up coming out having spent a fortune on stuff and it's too much. Instead:

1. Structure your puppy's day with a routine or timetable. Make time for play time but make sure you also schedule in rest time. Get your dog used to peace and quiet, it's like putting your baby down for a nap. They need to de-escalate and de-compress.
2. Ensure they have mental stimulation but don't over-stimulate them with those mind games from the pet shop. They're expensive and unnecessary.
3. Ignore any excessive whining and attention-seeking behaviours, rather than responding each time.

# CHAPTER 22

# RESOURCE GUARDING

'My dog snarls and growls if we go anywhere near her toy box. We need to curb her behaviour before she seriously hurts someone.'

Lunging Lottie, the Collie control freak, is making sure no one else gets her toys.

## Lottie's case file

**Dog's name:** Lottie
**Breed:** Collie
**Age:** 6
**Sex:** Female, neutered
**Owners:** Tracy and Dave

### Behavioural concerns?
- Resource guarding of toys
- Snarling to lunging within four months

### When did these behaviours start?
- Four months ago

**Previous training?**
- Tried taking toy box away

**How often is Lottie walked?**
- Twice per day

**What food do you feed?**
- Raw food

### 'Lottie was like Gollum with her Precious!'

Lottie's guarding of her toy box had become an obsessive-compulsive disorder. She was like Gollum with her Precious. She would get up, check the box, lie down, get up, check the box, lie down, constantly all day and night, wearing a path in the carpet! Dogs who resource guard will often focus on ONE toy and carry it around with them, putting it in their bed, or even guarding their bed. But Lottie wasn't doing this. It didn't need to be the ball that the owners were touching for her to go mad, it was anything in that whole area surrounding the toy box. The toy box was in the living room next to her bed and any time anyone walked past, she'd whine.

They'd tried moving the toy box out to the hallway but her behaviour had simply shifted so she'd started guarding the hall and they couldn't leave the front door! NOT IDEAL. Within four months, she had progressed from a whine to a growl, then a snarl, and then a full-on lunge if family members went anywhere near the toy box, which shows how quickly these things escalate if not dealt with. Tracy and Dave had kids, who were seven and twelve, so this really needed fixing.

# THE POWER OF THREE: Lottie's assessment

## 1. Diet
Lottie was already on a quality raw food diet so I knew that wasn't going to be the issue with her behaviour. Box ticked straight away!

## 2. Environment
Lottie's toy box was in the living room, right next to the TV and right next to her bed. The toy box was out all the time so she had full access to her toys whenever she wanted. Tracy first thought Lottie had an issue with the TV, that she didn't like the noise or something. That was the only connection she could make. But when she told me that she only started growling when the family moved towards the TV or stood up from the sofa to close the curtains or make a cup of tea, I realized it was the toy box.

## 3. Mental stimulation
Lottie was getting two walks a day but no mental stimulation. Mental stimulation is really important for working dogs like Collies. A lot of people get Collies from a litter at their local farm and they're not even one generation removed from working dogs. Ideally your dog would be two or three generations removed from working parents or you will need to do heaps of mental stimulation – agility, fly-ball, all those things.

---

### Lottie's 3-step guarding game plan

1. Change the layout of Lottie's living space.
2. Address her lack of mental stimulation and structured play time.
3. Take the toys away and reintroduce in a safe and structured way.

### How to fix your resource guarding rascal

Your dog could become obsessed with a toy, a slipper, glasses or the remote control, so how do YOU stop your dog resource guarding?

### Understand the issue

Resource guarding is about commodities. Owners often say to me, 'Oh she's protective over me, look how much she loves me' as their dog snaps and growls. And I have to burst their bubble and tell them it's not them being protective and showing they love you. They see you as a commodity, like a piece of food. They're guarding what they see as *theirs*, like toddlers who don't want to share and say, 'That's mine.' Lottie's whole purpose in life was to guard her toy box, like a full-time job. All she was missing was a little security paw-trol uniform!

### Identify the cause

I went through her toy box and got out all the toys one by one and that's how I realized that the true object of her affection was a blue squeaky ball, which Tracy had bought her four months earlier, just when this behaviour started. She got really excited and her eyes glazed over.

### Take the toys away

The first thing we had to do was take the toys away to keep the family safe. This is NOT to be confused with avoidance techniques. This is a specific thing where dogs' toys shouldn't be accessible to them 24/7, as we discuss in Chapter 3. They should only come out for play times and then be put away. We left the toy box where it was because we needed to get some other things in place before we could also remove that. Even though she knew the toys had been removed, the thing that she associated with her obsession was still there.

### Enrich her environment

We'd taken away the immediate danger but we risked giving Lottie mental health issues because she had lost the object of her obsession. HER PRECIOUS. Her only mental stimulation was her job of guarding the toy box and if we didn't enrich her life in another way, she would go crazy. I gave Tracy and Dave 48 hours to find a day care and book Lottie into some mental stimulation-style classes like agility, fly-ball or hydrotherapy. They got her into agility classes and day care.

## Monitor the obsession

I went back seven days later to see Lottie once she'd been to agility and day care. I'd asked Tracy and Dave to monitor her obsession with the toy box in that time. Within 72 hours of attending day care and agility classes, she had stopped getting up and checking the box every two minutes. She was still staring at it. She was VERY aware of it, sleeping with one eye open. But the obsession was removed by 75 per cent so I knew it was safe to remove the toy box completely.

## Muzzle training

If you have a dog who is obsessed with one toy, you need to do muzzle training (see Chapter 5 for more information), in order to remove things safely without your dog lunging or attacking. Alongside this, teach her the LEAVE command (see Chapter 4). Put her on a training lead in the house and place the item she guards on the floor out of her reach. Don't let her get too close to it. Say LEAVE. Once she's got this, move the item a bit closer and again ask her to LEAVE. Slowly get closer and closer.

## Shift her to a safe spot

We moved Lottie's bed away from the old spot by the TV to a new position behind the sofa so her guarding wouldn't become a habit. Her new place meant the family could safely come in and out of the living room and she was tucked away in the corner. We got a crate for her as well so she felt like she had her own little doggy den and she didn't feel threatened. You can read more about crate training in Chapter 5.

## Limit play time

As part of her mental stimulation schedule, we introduced half an hour play time twice a day. During these sessions we reintroduced Lottie's toys in a safe environment, making sure not to include the original ball or anything similar. These play times were the only access that Lottie had to her toys. After play time, they were tidied away out of sight and out of mind.

### Test for transference

What can sometimes happen is you take one toy away and your dog starts obsessing over another. This is called TRANSFERENCE. To prevent this, we had to carefully monitor Lottie's play time and if we had found her obsessing over another toy, we would step in and safely remove it.

### Pick a play area

Don't play with your dog's toys in the living room. Tracy and Dave had a large conservatory which led onto the garden so we made that the 'play area' for Lottie. She could run in and out if the weather was nice. You don't want the kitchen to be a playground because it's too dangerous and the living room is where you want peace and quiet in the evening.

### How's Lottie doing now?

Lottie loved agility and then they progressed to fly-ball because she was so good at it and the family really enjoyed doing it with her. Going from a family living in fear of their snarling dog, to one enjoying action-packed activities together was really heart-warming.

> 'Her only mental stimulation was her job of guarding the toy box!'

### 3 guarding mistakes you might be making

#### 1. Not giving your dog enough mental stimulation

For working dogs and their close descendants like Lottie, if you don't give them a job, they'll find one for themselves. Make sure you're taxing her brain as much as her physical strength each day.

### 2. Making a game of it

Your dog steals the remote control. You laugh. She cuddles it in her bed. Aww. Then she does it again and again. And now it's a pattern and she starts to get very defensive over it. So, you buy a new one. Let her have that one, you think. And now you have a dog that resource guards.

### 3. Letting fear stop you addressing the issue

If your dog has snarled or lunged at you, it's normal to feel scared. This can make owners fearful of addressing the issue but you can see how quickly these things escalate and action really does need taking ASAP.

### Leon's top tip

Watch out for early warning signs like stealing items from around the house and taking them to their bed – your glasses, the remote control, clothes from the washing pile. And always take the item off them. No matter how silly or harmless it seems. Don't encourage it or allow it to become a game. What starts as a silly game can manifest into serious OCD for your dog.

## Get it right from the start:
## Resource guarding training for puppies

Normally these cases start when they're a puppy so it's vital you know what to look out for and how to deal with this kind of behaviour.

1.  What seems cute in a puppy, a little growl or a nip, can become dangerous unwanted behaviour in an adult dog, so always address these kinds of issues as soon as they arise. It's like the seed is already planted.

2.  If you're buying a dog with two working parents, be aware that your dog will likely need to be a working dog too or need a LOT of mental stimulation. Factor this in when deciding the type of dog you want.

3.  Don't ever give your dog a bone from a butcher. People give their dogs marrow bones, dripping raw meat everywhere causing a hygiene risk, wrecking their teeth and becoming a choke hazard. You're giving the dog something of such high reward that would be the *crème de la crème*. You give them it and they take it to their bed so you're almost immediately creating this obsession.

# CHAPTER 23

# HUMPING

'My dog humps EVERYTHING. My best friend Doreen refuses to come to the house because she's so traumatized by Ellie's behaviour.'

Ellie is a passionate Pomeranian with a preference for doing it doggy style.

## Ellie's case file

**Dog's name:** Ellie
**Breed:** Pomeranian
**Age:** 8
**Sex:** Female, unneutered
**Owner:** Barbara

**Behavioural concerns?**
• Excessive humping of furniture, soft toys and people

**When did these behaviours start?**
• Always been frisky

**Previous training?**
• One trainer and one behaviourist, both said it was a sign of dominance

**What food do you feed?**
• Dry biscuits

## 'Every day was a HUMP day for this dog!'

This frisky Miss Minx Pomeranian was a pure nymph! She was humping the furniture, her soft toys and Barbara's friends when they came round to play Bridge. PUT DEREK DOWN, ELLIE! Barbara's best friend, Doreen, refused to come to the house anymore because she was so traumatized by Ellie's antics. Barbara told me that she had to shut Ellie out of the room when her church group visited because she'd have been all over them like a rash! This was a dog with a HIGH sex drive. As soon as I arrived, Ellie started making herself very COMFORTABLE on my leg. She had a tight grip for such a little thing. She was like a LEECH! Barbara was horrified and said, 'Our Ellie has always been frisky.' She was certainly not backwards at coming forwards, was she?! From the minute she got up in the morning, she was non-stop all day, HUMP-HUMP-HUMP. Every day was a HUMP day for this dog! Nothing was safe.

Barbara had tried plug-in pheromones recommended by the vet (they hadn't worked), she'd hidden all her soft toys, changed her bed from a lovely plush one to a rigid plastic one, and tried to break her sex trance while she was mid-flow by pulling her away from the object of her affection. But she still found her victims.

Most people who have dogs that love humping are told that they are trying to show dominance. But it's NOT THAT AT ALL. When your dog humps things, it is masturbating. Boy dogs do it, girl dogs do it. Barbara turned as pink as a flamingo when I told her that!

## THE POWER OF THREE: Ellie's assessment

### 1. Diet

Barbara had been told by a previous trainer to change Ellie's dry biscuit food because that was affecting it, which is something I had NEVER heard before. In this case, I didn't think the issue was being caused by her food, but Ellie DID need to be on a healthier, more balanced diet. Barbara didn't want to swap to raw food because her vet had convinced her she'd catch salmonella, based on no facts or research. EYE ROLL. We compromised and agreed to feed Ellie steam-pressed cooked food with at least 60 per cent meat content and no animal derivatives. For more diet advice, head to Chapter 3.

### 2. Environment

Ellie humped EVERYTHING – the sofa and soft furnishings, her bed, her toys, the kitchen table legs, Barbara's friends from church. You name it, Ellie would hump it. Barbara had changed Ellie's bed from a soft one to a hard plastic one, she'd changed her sofa to a wipe-clean leather version, she'd taken her soft toys away. She'd created a HUMP-PROOF house for Ellie with nothing soft for her to press herself up against. She was banned from upstairs because the bed would be a BIG NO-NO. Barbara did NOT want her desecrating that, thank you very much!

### 3. Mental stimulation

Ellie wasn't getting any mental stimulation. It was the other end she was stimulating. HELLO MATRON! Barbara was an elderly lady so she wasn't walking Ellie too far. She took her round the block or just let her out in the garden most days. She was also terrified that she'd CLAMP onto someone out on her walks. Ellie needed to be put on a sex-pest register! The lack of mental stimulation was a big factor because the humping had become a habit. Ellie couldn't stop even if she wanted to. A busy mind is a happy mind. With no soft toys, or walkies, what else was she meant to do with her time? OO-ER!

## Ellie's 3-step dirty dog plan

1. Day care three times per week – it's a
lot but she needed tiring out!
2. New healthy diet with no animal derivatives.
3. Neuter that naughty minx.

## How to fix your humping horror

Yes, it's embarrassing and 'awks' but we need to talk about masturbation (yes, really) and how YOU can get your dog to stop pestering your house guests and soft toys.

## Drain her brain

I asked Barbara if Ellie's humping had got worse since she'd taken her toys away and she said, 'Yes, MUCH worse!' I wasn't surprised because she'd taken away all her joy. She had nothing else to do but screw. We needed to tire Ellie out MENTALLY as well as physically. I recommended day care three times per week, which is a lot but she couldn't have soft toys in the house and we needed to exhaust her before we could try anything else. Ellie needed to attend day care for two weeks before I could return to try the training.

## Remove the toy triggers

In that space of time, we needed to make sure that Ellie didn't have access to any soft toys or a soft bed that she could have her wicked way with. We needed to restrict her access in the house as well so she couldn't bonk Barbara's bed.

## Forget dominant doggy style

I explained to Barbara that Ellie wasn't trying to dominate her when she was humping. This is an old-fashioned idea that is really common and completely FALSE. Why would your dog be trying to dominate the sofa, their soft toys, or their bed? It doesn't make sense. I told her that Ellie was getting sexually aroused by humping; essentially, she was masturbating. And she was masturbating ALL DAY. She was the dog equivalent of Samantha in *Sex and the City*. Barbara's face was a PICTURE. She was absolutely horrified, no doubt thinking about all the men and women in her circle who Ellie had had her wicked way with. She said, 'But she was doing it to my leg.' I KNOW BABS. STOP WEARING CHANEL!

## Don't encourage it

Normally humping becomes a funny party trick. I knew that wasn't the case for Barbara, who was an elderly woman with elderly friends. They weren't sitting around filming her for TikTok! But some owners accidentally encourage this behaviour if everyone laughs and watches because it rewards her with attention.

## Don't tell her off

Humping or masturbating is a natural thing for your dog to do so avoid telling her off. Barbara was pulling Ellie away from things and saying, 'STOP it!' Instead, gently brush her off and don't say anything. Dogs like Ellie won't even respond to verbal commands like OFF because their sex drive is so strong.

## Exhaust all options

When I went back to do the training, Ellie had been going to day care three times a week and was ABSOLUTELY KNACKERED. The mental stimulation had de-escalated the situation – she was masturbating 70 per cent less than she had been. We'd enriched her life and her humping had become less habitual because she was tired and her brain was busy. But the fact that she was still doing it proved that she was highly sexed and neutering her was the best option.

## Try chemical castration first

For bitches like Ellie, chemical castration is a good first step. It's an injection or pill which reduces her sex drive. By trying this first, before we neutered her, we could see if it had the desired effect. If it did, we'd go the whole hog and get her spayed. If it didn't work, it was reversable. No harm done. It worked and Barbara went ahead with making it permanent.

## How's Ellie doing now?

After she was spayed, Ellie completely stopped menacing the Bridge and Bible groups. She could have her soft toys again and a nice cosy bed, and Barbara's blushes were spared. She still goes to day care three days a week and she hasn't *totally* lost that twinkle in her eye.

'She was the dog equivalent of
Samantha in *Sex and the City*.'

---

### 3 minx-making mistakes you might be committing

**1. Giving her an audience**

If your dog humps and you laugh or encourage it in any way, you're going to create a habit which is really hard to shake. Instead, ignore her behaviour or take the steps outlined above.

**2. Offering no stimulation**

A busy brain is a happy brain. Dogs with too much time on their paws are more likely to hump out of boredom. They're desperate to stimulate SOMEthing.

**3. Rewarding bad behaviour**

Distracting your dog with a chew or a toy could signal a reward to them, encouraging them to do it even more.

---

## Leon's top tip

Try chemical castration first. This is available to male and female dogs and isn't permanent – it lasts for 6–12 months. I'd always do this first because if you go the whole hog and neuter or spay and then it's the wrong decision or it makes no difference to their behaviour, there's no going back. The chemical version allows you to trial it to see if it works first before going through the full procedure, as we see in Chapter 5.

## Get it right from the start: Sex Ed for puppies

Not all puppies or dogs hump but if your dog is showing signs, here's how to fix it.

1. Remove soft toys and just give them chew toys or rope toys instead.
2. Make sure you're giving your puppy enough mental stimulation and socialization.
3. Don't scold them for it. It's a natural urge and some dogs just have a higher sex drive than others.

# CHAPTER 24

# EXCESSIVE LICKING

'My dog licks constantly, especially when I have company. It has to stop. I'm awash in saliva!'

Say hello to Bodhi, the sensitive soul who loves to lick. All the time.

## Bodhi's case file

**Dog's name:** Bodhi
**Breed:** Tibetan Terrier
**Age:** 7
**Sex:** Male, neutered
**Owner:** Peter

**Behavioural concerns?**
- Excessive licking of paws and owner's hands

**When did these behaviours start?**
- Had always licked but last few months had got a lot worse

**Previous training?**
- One trainer that hadn't worked

**How often is Bodhi walked?**
- 2–3 times per day

**What food do you feed?**
- Wet food

> 'Dogs are so sensitive; they can tell when we're
> stressed and want to try to help us.'

Peter and his wife had just separated and before she moved out, there had been a lot of shouting and arguing in the house. Bodhi had always licked a bit but during this stressful time, his licking became excessive and non-stop. It reached an all-time high whenever Peter had company, especially women. It would set Bodhi off on three or four hours of licking. He licked his bed, the sofa, his paws and Peter's hands. There was a massive wet patch wherever he lay from the constant licking. Peter thought he was doing it for attention or because he didn't want other people being in the house.

Dogs lick to calm themselves down and some lick their owners to calm *them* down. Dogs are so sensitive; they can tell when we're stressed and want to try to help us.

## THE POWER OF THREE: Bodhi's assessment

### 1. Diet

With an issue like this, I immediately looked at the salt and yeast content of Bodhi's food. But in this case, it wasn't the food causing the issue. Peter was feeding him a good, clean, quality wet food.

## 2. Environment

Bodhi's behaviour had grown noticeably worse during the marriage break up. The constant arguing and shouting and subsequent frosty atmosphere had really affected Bodhi. Dogs are much more sensitive than we often give them credit for. Once Peter's ex had moved out, the house was a lot calmer. Bodhi had his own space and plenty of attention. He had always been an anxious dog and had always licked as a form of self-soothing.

## 3. Mental stimulation

Peter was walking Bodhi two or three times each day but nothing more. He told me that Bodhi loved swimming in the sea whenever he got the opportunity, which gave me an idea. Peter didn't want to take Bodhi to day care because he wanted whatever activity we chose for Bodhi to be something they shared together.

---

### Bodhi's 3-step lick-less plan

1. Get him checked for allergies, injuries and infections.
2. Tackle the licking trigger.
3. Inject a fun, endorphin-rich activity into his life to replace the licking.

---

## How to fix your lick-happy dog

A dog that endlessly licks can be a real pain and embarrassing when you have company. Let's look at how YOU can train your dog to lick less.

## Get him checked by the vet

My first port of call was the vet. Did Bodhi have an allergy? Or an infection? Had he injured himself? All these things can cause a dog to lick like this. If your dog is excessively licking his private parts, he could have a water infection. People just shout, 'Stop licking your bits' but there could be something wrong. Yeast infections can be brought on by poor diet with too much salt and yeast. This often shows up inside a dog's ears. They would be scratching their ears and licking their paws, transferring the poison out of their ears onto their paws and back round again. Bodhi got the all clear from the vet.

### Find the issue

When dogs lick like this it's a form of self-soothing. They do it to calm themselves. Bodhi was feeling anxious with the change in the household dynamic, which is what led to the excessive licking as he fought to soothe his anxiety. But he was also trying to calm Peter down. He would lick his hand more when Peter had female company. QUITE THE MOOD KILLER. It was so sweet to think of Bodhi trying to soothe Peter. I got quite teary thinking about it.

### Tackle the trigger

In Bodhi's case, the trigger was women because of the arguing that had happened between Peter and his ex-wife. When Peter brought women round for a date, Bodhi would expect a massive row and it would destabilize him, sky-rocketing his anxiety and leading him to lick. I explained to Peter that it was the smell of the women. Bodhi could smell the oestrogen and their perfume and that would trigger his behaviour. Bodhi was licking for a reason and the licking was an EXTERNAL symptom. If we had just stopped him licking, without addressing WHY, it would have become internal and he would have had no release, which would have dramatically affected his mental health.

### Channel fun to ease his anxiety

Because Bodhi loved swimming in the sea, I suggested hydrotherapy for them twice a week to give Bodhi plenty of mental stimulation and an outlet other than licking. It was also something they could do together. Peter wanted to be part of whatever was enriching Bodhi's life. Swimming in the warm water would release masses of endorphins to help Bodhi feel calm and give him that feel-good factor and a natural high, which would all reduce his need to lick. When a dog swims, he uses his brain the entire time because he has to really concentrate to move all four limbs.

### Plan ahead

Because we knew that Bodhi's trigger was women in the house, when Peter started dating his new girlfriend and wanted her to meet Bodhi, I suggested he take her along to the hydrotherapy session before she came to the house. That way Bodhi could meet her on neutral, non-threatening ground and she could help Bodhi turn a negative trigger into a positive experience. He would start to associate Peter's new partner with swimming, his HAPPY place.

### Never use a deterrent or punishment to stop licking

One trainer had told Peter to use window cleaner on his hands to prevent Bodhi licking them! It's POISON! Can you imagine!? Other 'solutions' I've heard people suggest are Tabasco sauce, mustard, chilli powder and peri peri sauce. Using these is a form of PUNISHMENT. It can cause injury, burning a dog's taste buds and their tongue, which can damage your dog permanently! It doesn't STOP the licking. They'll just go and do it somewhere else.

### How's Bodhi doing now?

The excessive licking has stopped! His home is now a peaceful, loving environment, which suits Bodhi really well. Peter and Bodhi still go to hydrotherapy twice a week and often take Peter's girlfriend with them.

'I suggested hydrotherapy for them twice a week to give Bodhi plenty of mental stimulation and an outlet other than licking.'

## 3 let-him-lick mistakes you might be making

### 1. Feeding him a diet high in yeast or salt
Check your dog's diet and get him looked over by your vet to rule out allergies or infections.

### 2. Stopping your dog licking if he's stressed
If your dog is stressed or anxious, he might lick to calm himself down. Interrupting this without giving him another outlet could be damaging.

### 3. Putting him in a high-stress environment
Relationships break down and dogs can get caught in the middle. While you might have other priorities, don't forget your dog and how loud arguments and fighting can affect him.

## Leon's top tip

Harness your dog's natural love of licking by using it to build your connection. Buy a doggy ice cream or sorbet, and let him lick it out of the tub while you hold it. It's a fantastic bonding session, especially if he's a rescue or nervous dog or if he's a dog you don't really know and you want to build up trust with.

## Get it right from the start: Bonding training for puppies
If you have an anxious pup, or you just want to increase your connection, try these things.

1. Schedule a licking session once a week to help you bond with him. Buy a doggy ice cream or sorbet and spend time holding it for him. He sees the tub as an extension of you so it floods him with positive thoughts.
2. Flavour some ice cubes by puréeing some lovely fruit and vegetables, mixing with water and freezing them. Hold one in your hand for your dog to lick.
3. Get your puppy to bond with visitors by asking your visitor to hold a doggy ice cream and get them to do the bonding exercise with the dog. It builds trust and gets your puppy happy around visitors.

# CHAPTER 25

# GROWLING

'My dog bit my son. If we can't get her to stop, we'll have to rehome her.'

Rosie the bolshy Boxer doesn't like change and is willing to throw her weight around to get her own way.

## Rosie's case file

**Dog's name:** Rosie
**Breed:** Boxer
**Age:** 12
**Sex:** Female, neutered
**Owners:** Karen, a single mum, and her teenage son Jamie

### Behavioural concerns?
- Growling and biting on the sofa

### When did these behaviours start?
- They'd escalated over many years

**Previous training?**
* None

**What food do you feed?**
* Dry kibble

### 'We had to teach Rosie that the sofa was not HERS.'

Karen phoned me up crying, saying she needed to rehome Rosie because she'd bitten her son, Jamie. He'd tried to move her from her spot on the sofa and she'd nipped him and drawn blood. Rosie was being confronted and she had to react to get her own way. She hadn't wanted to HURT him. No dog WANTS to be aggressive.

Rosie had always had a blanket on the sofa, which was HER place. Karen had bought a new sofa and moved the blanket and it evidently was NOT to Madame Rosie's liking. So even though the blanket wasn't in her normal place, she tried to go back to her old spot. When Jamie tried to move her, she'd turned nasty. Rosie had always growled and grumbled when they'd disturbed her on the sofa or on Karen's bed, where she slept. Poor Karen couldn't roll over in bed for fear of waking Rosie and her wrath! Time to change your bed time companion Karen! Karen and Jamie had always made excuses for her. And let her GET AWAY WITH IT. Without even seeing Rosie, I knew immediately how to fix the problem. I told Karen it could be fixed with minimum fuss within a couple of weeks. Although biting is serious, I told Karen that if anyone needed rehoming it was HER not Rosie! You can't rehome a 12-year-old dog who's been with you her entire life because of a problem YOU have caused. It's not fair.

## THE POWER OF THREE: Rosie's assessment

### 1. Diet
Rosie was fed a run-of-the-mill dog biscuit diet but it wasn't the food that was causing her aggression. To help her into old age, we put her on a higher-quality cooked food. And to help with her arthritis I added green-lipped mussel as a supplement to her diet (see Chapter 3).

### 2. Environment
At night Rosie slept upstairs on Karen's bed. It was a lovely king size comfy memory foam mattress with layered blankets, but it was very inconvenient having to share with a human. In the day time she was on her favourite old blanket on the new sofa, which she wasn't so keen on. Her actual dog bed was a hard plastic thing with a blanket in it in the living room and Karen said, 'She's got a dog bed there and she never uses it.' I said, 'I wouldn't use it either. What would you go for, this horrible cold hard thing or a lovely squashy sofa or bed?'

### 3. Mental stimulation
Rosie had arthritis so they weren't doing loads with her. Karen thought that because she was an older dog she wouldn't change and was beyond hope. WRONG!

---

### Rosie's 3-step bolshy Boxer plan

1. Get Rosie checked out at the vet in case her aggression is being caused by pain.
2. Swap the seductive sofa for a five-star heated doggy bed.
3. Set new bed time boundaries for our bolshy Boxer.

### How to fix your cross-patch canine

Whether your dog has nipped you or whether she is at the growling stage, this kind of aggressive behaviour in the house needs nipping (sorry!) in the bud. Let's look at how YOU can prevent your dog calling all the shots.

### Get her checked out

I told Karen to take Rosie to the vets to rule out any pain caused by her arthritis or other issues. Pain can make dogs grumpy and snappy, the same as humans. Coming from a hydrotherapy background, I knew what pain medication Rosie could have and the levels she should be having and wanted to make sure she was on the right stuff. Rosie was given the all clear.

### Tackle that teenage behaviour

Rosie's moody attitude was the equivalent of Karen having ANOTHER teenager in the house. She was being confrontational, trying to take ownership of the house, throwing her weight around and dominating the environment. AND IT HAD TO STOP. When we live together, we have to RESPECT each other's boundaries and spaces.

### Stop making excuses

It had started with a growl, when Karen had tried to move Rosie. She'd done that a few times, shown her teeth, given her the full GRUMPSVILLE attitude – 'She's in a right mood tonight.' Then the next time she had tried to move her, Rosie had snarled because her growling hadn't worked. And over time, Karen had become scared of getting bitten, so she'd avoided moving her. That had shown Rosie that her behaviour – growling and snarling – had had the desired effect because she got left alone on her comfy sofa. There were no more confrontations. JOB DONE. But then they'd got a new sofa and Jamie had to move her to sit down. And because her old growling hadn't worked, she'd had to ESCALATE it so she'd be left alone. She'd lunged and bitten him. She'd been conditioned over the years that this aggressive behaviour worked. As owners, we need to remember that when it's a growl, it's already gone too far. If it's a lunge or a nip, then it's definitely gone too far.

### No more sofa surfing

I told Karen that we needed to get Rosie OFF THE SOFA. Not because I have an issue with dogs being on the sofa, I don't. I used to love having Scooby watching TV next to me. A lot of behaviourists say, 'Dogs shouldn't be on the furniture. They should be on the floor.' They say it's a dominance thing and that the dog thinks she's human. I'm NOT saying that. Dogs can be on the furniture if they're INVITED onto it. We had to teach Rosie that the sofa was not HERS. We did this by saying no sofa for TWO WEEKS. She wasn't allowed on for even five minutes. If she got up, Karen had to get her OFF.

### Teach her new commands

We taught Rosie to get off the furniture using the UP and OFF commands. Karen was understandably scared to get Rosie off the sofa so we put a puppy training lead on her. When Karen wanted to get her off the bed or sofa, we'd say OFF and use the lead to gently guide her off. We didn't tug or yank it.

### Give her somewhere of her own

To replace the sofa, and because of her arthritis, we got Rosie a lovely orthopaedic mattress, which was good for her joints. You can get them heated as well! Five-star treatment for our Rosie! This mattress helped alleviate her pain, and was WAY more beneficial to her than being on the sofa. The idea was that she'd prefer to sleep on her new mattress anyway. Everyone needs comfort in old age.

### Invite her onto the sofa and tell her when she's outstayed her welcome

After the two-week sofa ban, we looked at how Karen could INVITE Rosie onto the sofa. It had to be KAREN'S decision, not Rosie's. I told Karen to keep the training lead on so we could easily get her off when we wanted to. The last thing we wanted to do was take the lead off and leave Karen in a vulnerable situation. Karen said UP and Rosie got up and could lie there, do whatever she wanted, but when Karen told her to get OFF, she had to get off. I reinforced to Karen that it was HER space. She wouldn't invade Rosie's bed – although with that heated mattress it was *verrrry* tempting! Karen had to restrict how long Rosie was on the sofa for those first few weeks. Only 15 minutes at a time, otherwise things would slip and Rosie would revert back to the old behaviour.

### Avoid humanizing your dog

Don't humanize your dog and think, 'Oh it's really cruel, we haven't let her on the sofa' because dogs don't think like that. Rosie's new bed was the *crème de la crème*. Never mind the sofa, get me curled up on the orthopaedic! Don't get caught up in the whole guilt thing. You shouldn't force your dog to be in your space constantly.

### Don't make your bed

A lot of people lie in bed with their dog on the duvet and they sleep in weird positions because they don't want to move the dog. NO. I DON'T THINK SO. Poor Karen was pinned to the bed. If she rolled over in the night, Rosie would growl and snarl. Not a relaxing sleep environment. I don't have an issue with dogs being on the bed but I DO have an issue with them growling at you when you roll over or move. If your dog behaves like Rosie, you've got to get her OFF THE BED.

### Set new bedroom boundaries

Karen couldn't monitor where Rosie was in the bedroom while she was asleep. Rosie might start off on HER OWN bed and then migrate to Karen's. And then she'd be in a vulnerable situation. We had to banish Rosie from the bedroom. Karen said, 'She likes sleeping with me' and I asked how she knew that because she shut her in so Rosie had no option but to sleep there. She might have been desperate to get out – 'Maybe you snore and she hates it! You're holding her captive.' Instead, Rosie needed her OWN area downstairs. At bedtime we moved her new bed from the living room to the kitchen so she couldn't just jump straight onto the sofa the minute she had the run of the living room. We're onto you Rosie!

### Let sleeping dogs lie

If your dog is FAST asleep on the sofa, DO NOT suddenly grab them to get them off. If someone came into your bedroom in the middle of the night when you were asleep and ripped your duvet off and grabbed you out of bed, how would you feel? I think you'd have something to say! Shock can make some dogs snap. Try to avoid being in this situation but, if you do need to move them, put a lead on and do it in a non-confrontational way.

## How's Rosie doing now?

Everyone is happier. Everyone's fingers are in one piece. There were no more issues and there was no more talk of rehoming. After dinner, Karen invites Rosie up for a cuddle and then she puts Netflix on and Rosie gets down and has her own space on her lovely little luxury bed. Lucky Rosie!

'A lot of people lie in bed with their dog on the duvet and they sleep in weird positions because they don't want to move the dog. NO. I DON'T THINK SO.'

### 3 cranky canine mistakes you might be making

#### 1. Making excuses
Every time you excuse your dog saying she's grumpy or tired, or cranky or old, you are REINFORCING her unwanted behaviour. And it *will* escalate.

#### 2. Using your dog as an emotional crutch
Does your dog love to sleep on your bed with you, or is it actually you that wants *her* company? Don't humanize your dog to make yourself feel better.

#### 3. Giving your dog a blanket on the sofa
As soon as you give them a space like that, they will guard it. Make sure they have a nice comfy bed of their own and if you want them on the sofa or your bed, INVITE them up for a limited time, then get them OFF.

### Leon's top tip

We all make excuses for our best friends – and our dogs are no different. But making excuses can let unwanted behaviour THRIVE, putting you and your dog in danger. Stepping in at an early stage is FAR easier than having to call in the big guns when things have deteriorated past the point of no return. Think firm but fair.

## Get it right from the start:
## Behaviour training for puppies

We love sharing our homes with our dogs but make sure everyone is on the same page from the start.

1. Don't put a blanket on the sofa for your puppy. You're giving them a space to guard and creating a problem that didn't need to be there.
2. Respect each other's space like children and parents do. It's not about who's in charge or the pecking order but living in mutual respect. Dogs, like teenagers, need their own space.
3. Teach your puppy UP and OFF and invite her onto the furniture if that's what you want to do.

# CHAPTER 26

# DOG-ON-DOG DOMINANCE

'My dog is dominant with other dogs and pins them to the ground like a WWE wrestler. How can we repair our reputation?'

Unruly Rupert loves to try his wrestling moves on unsuspecting dogs.

## Rupert's case file

**Dog's name:** Rupert
**Breed:** Husky
**Age:** 18 months
**Sex:** Male, neutered
**Owners:** Kim and Josie

### Behavioural concerns?
• Jumping on other dogs and pinning them to the ground

### When did these behaviours start?
• Puppy

**Previous training?**
• None

**How often is Rupert walked?**
• Twice per day

**What food do you feed?**
• Dry beef kibble supplemented with red meat (steaks, burgers, sausages)

### 'Rupert was like a mafia don putting other dogs in their place to make up for his lack of confidence!'

Rupert was an intense character who would grab intact male dogs by the neck, pull them to the ground and pin them down, as if to say, 'I'm the boss round here' like a mafia don. He would then leave them and walk off. It was over in a matter of seconds but it could be incredibly traumatizing for the other dog. Rupert did this whether he was on the lead or off and it was happening six or SEVEN times each walk, leaving a trail of destruction and annoyed dog owners behind him. His owners Kim and Josie weren't really dealing with his behaviour because they didn't think he was doing anything wrong! I was shocked but that's what a lot of people's attitudes are. 'He's not biting them, it's play fighting. He's just pulling them down and standing over them. He's not harming them,' they said. Imagine if a human did that, a full-on wrestling move on a stranger! The last time it happened, they were told by a fellow dog owner that if they didn't deal with Rupert's aggressive behaviour, she was going to report them.

Nine times out of ten, a dominant dog like Rupert lacks confidence which manifests as aggression. It's CLASSIC bully behaviour. He only ever went for entire male dogs. PURE JEALOUS. This was a dog that needed some zen in his life.

## THE POWER OF THREE: Rupert's assessment

### 1. Diet

Rupert was on a red meat kibble diet – lamb, beef and duck – which was feeding his aggression. This needed to change FAST.

### 2. Environment

Rupert's home life was fine because there were no other intact males around, but the minute they went outside, he was on the prowl looking for his next victim. Because Kim and Josie weren't addressing the problematic behaviour, he was getting worse. They were pariahs in the local area with people crossing the road to avoid them, and leaving the park.

### 3. Mental stimulation

Rupert was getting no mental stimulation other than his daily walks. No local doggy day cares would take him. He'd had THREE separate trial days at different places and they'd all BANNED him for his bad behaviour and failing their assessments. No one would schedule play dates with them because their reputation preceded them.

---

### Rupert's 3-step anti-aggro plan

1. Get rid of the red meat for a less aggression-heavy alternative.
2. Address the dominance problem responsibly via muzzle training.
3. Teach him how to speak dog at day care.

---

### How to fix your dominant dog

It's really important for everyone's safety that you deal with dog-on-dog dominance safely. Follow the simple steps below to help fix YOUR dog.

### Take it seriously

I had harsh words with Kim and Josie and told them that Rupert's behaviour could be damaging other dogs and leading *them* to fear aggression because they've been randomly attacked. They tried to correct me and said, 'He's not attacking them though, is he?' I said, 'Yes he IS.' If that was a work environment, you'd be getting sacked unless you were a bloody sumo wrestler!

### Remove the red meat

We needed to remove red meat from Rupert's diet. They were cooking him mince and steaks and whenever they had a family barbecue, they were chucking him burgers and sausages. Red meat constantly. That was what they thought a dog should have. I put Rupert onto a raw chicken and turkey diet. I told them to do this for four weeks before we began training.

### Say no to early neutering

Unfortunately, when Rupert was just a year old, their vet had told Kim and Josie to neuter him. BAD ADVICE. They shouldn't have even considered neutering him until he was at least 18 months old. We look at neutering in detail in Chapter 5. Neutering him too early removed his one source of confidence – testosterone – and made his dominance problem a million times worse. If you think being intact could be causing your dog's dominant behaviour, you can try chemical castration as a non-permanent option.

### Muzzle training

Getting Rupert to respect other dogs in a safe way could only be achieved through muzzle training. Kim and Josie were resistant, saying, 'People will think he's dangerous and will avoid us.' I told them that people were avoiding them anyway because their reputation round those parts was worse than Jack the Ripper's! I told them that muzzle training (see Chapter 5 for more details) was the ONLY option. If they didn't agree, I couldn't help them.

### Let him know what's acceptable and what isn't

Rupert had no idea that his antics were unacceptable because Kim and Josie had happily let him go up to other dogs with the attitude that it was better to get it over with. Once he'd pinned the other dog, he'd move on! WHAT THE HELL? But I wasn't letting that happen. I needed Rupert to be calm around other dogs with testosterone and to understand that pinning a dog is NOT an acceptable way to say hello.

### Find some friends

I put out a Facebook request in their area asking for meet ups with people who had entire male dogs that were non-reactive and friendly. I wanted to introduce Rupert to non-threatening dogs in a safe environment to help create a connection with entire dogs. I needed the right mix – different ages, breeds, colours, submissive, entire males. It was QUITE the shopping list!

### Turn the negative trigger into a positive

I shortlisted three dogs in the area who fit the criteria we needed. If I could make sure that Rupert had a good experience with those dogs and it was done correctly, then we could overcome his dominant behaviour. With these three dogs we did the same process as for fear aggression on the lead (see Chapter 19) where we had Rupert licking a block of Brussels pâté on the lead while looking at these dogs. We met a different dog per week and it never lasted more than 15 minutes and was always in my presence.

### Take it slow and steady

In the first training session, Rupert wasn't interested in the pâté. AT ALL. Even just the scent of testosterone from the other dog sent him BONKERS. He was fixated. The following week he was more relaxed, licking the pâté. Even just licking it once showed me he was able to let his guard down. And it got better each time. It was a slow process but we couldn't turn back the clock and un-castrate him. Slowly and surely would win the race. After three weeks and three dogs, we changed over back to the original dog, and we did that for the next three months.

### Progress at their pace

Three months later, once Rupert was comfortable in the presence of the other entire males and could be within 50m (164ft) of them, we put his muzzle on and started walking them on leads towards each other with a 10m (33ft) gap between them. This mimicked crossing paths with another dog while out walking, but they never got to meet up close. We did this five or six times and once Rupert showed he was happy and displayed no aggressive behaviour, I took one of the training dogs in one hand and Rupert (still wearing his muzzle) in the other and walked them side by side. They were still separate with me in the middle but they walked in the same direction.

### Dial in doggy day care

Once we'd got Rupert to this stage, I knew he could start going to our day care. He started two days a week. I was super careful about who he was with. I didn't want to set him back by putting him in with a bolshy entire male brimming with confidence, or have him traumatize another dog. He needed to build up good relationships with his peer group and learn how to speak dog, something only other dogs could teach him.

### How's Rupert doing now?

He's still a work in progress. We've built his confidence up to remove the threat that entire males pose to him. Rupert built up a rapport with the three dogs that Kim and Josie were able to meet up and practise with. They walked him side by side with them. It's not a quick fix because his behaviour had been allowed for so long. If we hadn't done this, Rupert wouldn't have been able to interact with his own species and would have been starved of any play with his peer group. We had to overcome it.

### 'He needed to build up good relationships with his peer group and learn how to speak dog.'

## 3 dominant dog mistakes you might be making

### 1. Thinking it's acceptable behaviour
Just because the dog that is pinned to the ground isn't *physically* injured doesn't mean it's not mentally damaged from being attacked out of the blue. It could end up with fear aggression towards other dogs, which is very serious.

### 2. Upping their aggression
Feeding your dominant dog red meat will simply increase their aggression. Instead, swap to white meat or fish alternatives.

### 3. Make time for mental stimulation
If your dominant dog isn't allowed into day care, you need to make sure you're structuring mental stimulation for him – this could be games, structured play time or an activity like hydrotherapy.

### Leon's top tip

Go easy when judging other dog owners. If you see a dog wearing a muzzle, take into account they might be training or rehabilitating their dog and don't just assume their dog is nasty or that the owner is cruel. They are taking all precautions to make sure that the public are safe.

## Get it right from the start: Dominance training for puppies
Don't let having a dominant puppy ruin your dog walks.

1. Socialize your puppy from the start. He might need to wear a muzzle and that's fine.

2. If your puppy displays traits like pinning other dogs or grabbing them by the neck, consider it a warning and seek help. If it shows up in a puppy, it will escalate.

3. Deal with the problem BEFORE you neuter your dog. And if neutering seems the only option, try chemical castration first as it's temporary.

CHAPTER 27

# ATTACKING CARS, BIKES AND RUNNERS

'My dog attacks every car, cyclist and runner he sees. We're terrified he's going to get hurt or cause an accident. Help!'

Toby's trick is to terrorize passing motorists, cyclists and runners by lunging at them to make them disappear.

---

## Toby's case file

**Dog's name:** Toby
**Breed:** Doberman
**Age:** 1
**Sex:** Male, unneutered
**Owners:** Darren and Craig

**Behavioural concerns?**
• Lunging at cars, bikes, runners

**When did these behaviours start?**
- Since they moved house

**Previous training?**
- None

**How often is Toby walked?**
- Twice per day round the park, avoiding roads (they are scared he'd get run over)

**What food do you feed?**
- Dry biscuits

'I told them to IMMEDIATELY get rid of the extendable lead – they burn my eyes!'

When Darren and Craig moved house, they were excited for all the new dog walks they could take Toby on. The local park was a short walk away along a busy road. But the first time they walked along the road, Toby leaped out like a dog POSSESSED, barking at the passing cars and almost dragging Craig in front of a lorry. A bit much for a Sunday afternoon walk! They swiftly turned for home, badly shaken.

After that they had tried walking Toby earlier in the day to avoid the traffic but they found that there were more cyclists and runners and he was lunging at them as well. Toby did not like anything moving past him. Every time they took Toby out, he lunged into the road and his owners were understandably scared to walk him. Before the move, Darren and Craig had never walked Toby along a road so they didn't realize he had a problem. It didn't even come into their heads to consider roads when they bought the new house.

## THE POWER OF THREE: Toby's assessment

### 1. Diet

Toby was on a diet of dry kibble. The food was full of carbs which turn to sugar causing hyperactivity so I knew that was a MAJOR problem. They didn't want to do the raw diet because Darren was a vegetarian so we did good-quality steam-cooked food with 70 per cent meat, 30 per cent vitamins and vegetables. Toby was far too hyperactive to do anything until he'd been on the new diet for two weeks.

### 2. Environment

Everything in Toby's house was absolutely fine. It was the house's LOCATION that was causing this issue. Moving house can unsettle your dog and it's important to think about the area surrounding your house. Is there a park nearby? Do you have to walk on a road? Is there a pavement to walk your dog safely? Toby had never been walked along roads so being confronted by loud, fast cars and trucks, cyclists whizzing past and runners springing out of nowhere, totally unnerved him causing a BIG reaction.

### 3. Mental stimulation

Toby socialized with other dogs regularly on play dates and had plenty of time in the garden playing with his toys.

---

### Toby's 3-step traffic terror plan

1. Get a safer lead – non-extendable – and learn how to use it.
2. Desensitize him to traffic and moving objects
in a calm and safe environment.
3. Cement his new normal with weekend walkies
to the park and cycle track.

## How to fix your traffic terrorist

It's super important to fix this issue quickly because it's not just your dog who is in danger, but you or whoever walks him, and there's also the strong chance of him causing an accident through his behaviour. Let's look at how YOU can train your dog to respect traffic calmly and confidently.

### Fight the fear

Roads are quite scary for dogs, with a lot of sensory overload – loud noises, visual stimulation, the whoosh of a fast car, a bus with air brakes. All of these things have the potential to startle your dog. Lunging at traffic stems from FEAR. Darren and Craig were completely unaware of their surroundings and how they might affect Toby.

### Let the extendable lead go

We went for a walk to the park so I could see the problem for myself and it was REALLY BAD. Toby was lunging and pulling towards anything that moved, jumping around the path, into the road, back again. Craig was walking him on an extendable lead, flapping in the breeze like your grandma's washing. Toby was in and out, in and out, weaving in front of him, around him, behind him. There was no order at all. It was a total FREE FOR ALL. Even if Toby hadn't been scared of traffic, the way he was walking him would have been dangerous and needed sorting. I told them to IMMEDIATELY get rid of the extendable lead – they burn my eyes! I hate them so much.

### Take the inside track

After I'd given them a BOLLOCKING, I asked if they would walk their niece and nephew down the road without holding their hand. OF COURSE NOT. So WHY did I witness them walking Toby on an extendable lead which wasn't locked, right next to the road? It doesn't occur to people to walk their dog on the inside – away from the traffic – to keep them safe and prevent them getting scared. Use your body to block the traffic and protect your pooch.

### Don't verge on the ridiculous

In the UK there are a lot of pavements with the grass verge next to the road, which is a problem because people let their dogs roam on the grass. Like lots of other owners before them, Darren and Craig told me that Toby only liked walking on the grass verge, not the pavement. YOU DIDN'T TELL ME HE COULD SPEAK ENGLISH! I've worked with dogs for 14 years and none of them has ever spoken to me. They laughed and I said, 'You've humanized him and YOU'VE decided that he prefers the grass. To keep him safe, you need to keep him OFF the verge and AWAY from the road.'

### Learn on-the-lead manners

Even after two weeks and a new lead (THANK GOD), Darren and Craig's lead skills still left a LOT TO BE DESIRED. They were letting Toby cross in front of them, they were complaining about having a sore arm from having to pull him in to the side all the time. CRY ME A RIVER. They were tripping over him as he crossed onto the grass verge. I explained that a dog should never cross over in front of you. Your arm should be relaxed and down by your side as we discussed in lead training in Chapter 5. Toby was choking because he was pulling so much, so we changed him to a TRIANGLE split lead, which took the pressure off his neck and made a huge difference to how much control Craig and Darren had (see Chapter 17 for more detail on this method).

### Do desensitization training

After two weeks of the new lower-carb diet, we did desensitization training. I asked Darren and Craig to organize a play date earlier in the day to tire Toby out so we could begin in a relaxed frame of mind. I found a bus stop in their village which was set back a little way from the road but still had plenty going on. It was quiet enough to do the desensitization without flooding Toby with fear. That's the last thing we wanted to do because then he'd just be TERRIFIED. I told them to come to this bus stop every day at quiet times – mid-morning or mid-afternoon – and just sit there with Toby either down at their feet or on the bench next to them. Let him watch and see people getting on and off the bus, the odd car going past. It had to be in the day time and not the dark because dogs can be scared of the dark. They had to not make too much fuss of him because that would feed into his anxiety.

### Ignore the behaviour

During this time, Darren and Craig were to ignore any lunging or growling at traffic or moving things because we hadn't actually started any training. They did this for four weeks, once a day for 30 minutes, and it started to pay off.

### Banish the bike blues

Once I knew Toby was calm at the bus stop, we pushed him a little further. We took him to the park at the weekend and met up with a friend of theirs who had a bicycle. Darren and Craig knew him but Toby didn't. It was important to use someone that the dog doesn't know because I wanted him focused on the bicycle, not the person. We did the DRIP-FEED tactic with Brussels pâté, which we cover in more detail in Chapter 19. We stood 50m (164ft) away from the cyclist, put the visual in front of Toby, and let him lick the pâté. Then we got him to step forward and get closer and closer that way. Toby did so well.

### Rein in fear of runners

Lots of dogs have issues with runners. It's not that your dog doesn't like runners, it's the fact that they suddenly creep up from nowhere behind them or they come flying around a corner wearing hi-vis and your dog gets a fright. Dogs are often scared of hi-vis jackets because they temporarily blind them. The light hits the hi-vis and he can't see.

### Find your new normal

Darren and Craig had ongoing training to do with Toby. Every Saturday they had to walk Toby to the park with the cycle track and let him watch the cyclists go by for 15 minutes. They were to give him a chew or high-value treat to help cement his new normal of being fine with moving things.

## How's Toby doing now?

Toby is doing great and the family have settled into their new home. We managed to turn terrified-of-traffic Toby into a dog who walks nicely on the lead next to busy roads in under three months. INCREDIBLE. Darren and Craig could have many happy years with Toby – I've known dogs live to be 23 – three months of training is nothing.

> 'Dogs are often scared of hi-vis jackets because they temporarily blind them.'

### 3 traffic mistakes you might be making

**1. Pulling on the lead**

You should never pull or yank on the lead. It can really damage a dog's neck muscles and give him whiplash. It will only make him pull even harder.

**2. Using avoidance techniques**

Avoidance techniques don't *solve* the problem. If you're driving to the park instead of walking, not walking them at all or letting them out in the garden to toilet, or hiding behind cars or walls if you spot a cyclist, runner or car, then you're avoiding. Stop. You need to FIX the problem.

**3. Pushing them too far**

A lot of people are told to take their dog to a busy street and sit there but it's too much for them. They're already terrified of one car going past, never mind 20. It's too much. You could cause more damage in the long run by making them so terrified that they go to attack whatever it is. Start slow and small. Increase gradually.

## Leon's top tip

Buy a hi-vis vest and leave it around the house in
random places such as the back of a chair or on the sofa.
If your dog has seen one around the house, they won't panic
as much when they're out and see one in the 'wild'.

## Get it right from the start:
## Traffic training for puppies

Getting your puppy used to all the different kinds of road noises and vehicles is really important for their future.

1. Properly socialize your dog – take him to the park and get him to see runners, bikes, children on scooters, prams, wheelchairs, skateboards, rollerblades – it's an enriching area for a dog to be. As soon as they've had their second injections, you should be taking your puppy to these places.
2. Get him used to traffic safely – make sure he's on a short lead, keep him on the inside, and walk him around different kinds of traffic so he's used to lorries, cars, buses and motorbikes from an early age.
3. If you have friends who have bikes or are runners, you could ask them to do a short training exercise where they cycle or run past your pup. It's important he understands what all the different noises and visuals are.

# Part 3: Final Thoughts

## One last thing before you go

You've got the theory and changed your mindset, you've worked through the firsthand case studies to put the theory into practice, you're ready! But before you go, know that I've got your back. If your training plan stops being effective or your dog develops a different problem, you can come back to this section and go through the Troubleshooting checklist.

Always reset and ask the BASICS. Go back to the Power of Three. What have you missed? What is your dog telling you if only you'd listen?

Once that's all sorted, I look at the hardest part of having a dog, losing your best friend. My experience with Scooby was sudden. And it FLOORED me. Everyone's experience will be different but there are some universal truths that are the same for us ALL. Although no one wants to think about it, I want you to be as prepared as you can be, and to learn from my mistakes.

# CHAPTER 28

# TROUBLESHOOTING CHECKLIST

I want you to use this book as your dog's life manual. Something you can rely on again and again. You might have picked it up to solve one challenging issue and got that problem sorted, then further down the line, your dog might do something else that you need to fix. You can pick this book up again and find real ANSWERS.

Just flip to the relevant chapter and get to work! What are you waiting for?

If your dog's challenging behaviour isn't responding to your bespoke training plan, go back to basics: THE POWER OF THREE. Every issue *always* comes back to at least one of these three things:

1. DIET
2. ENVIRONMENT
3. MENTAL STIMULATION

I recommend working through each topic, thinking about what you might have missed or what the reason might be for your dog's behaviour or his inability to understand. Use the checklist to help. These are just some of the questions – and by no means an exhaustive list – that you can ask yourself if your dog doesn't respond to training.

Remember these things can take time. You can't judge your dog on how quickly someone else's dog got the hang of things. Make sure your training is consistent but don't overdo it.

I know how much you love your dog and want the best for him. I know you can do it! And remember: dogs WANT to please and there is *always* a reason for their unwanted behaviour.

---

## Checklist

Try using the checklist below to help.

- ☑ Has the vet checked him over for illness or injuries?
- ☑ Have you checked what is in your dog's diet?
- ☑ Is he getting the right amount of food?
- ☑ Is he getting too many carbs or too much red meat?
- ☑ Could you swap him to a healthier raw diet?
- ☑ What about his treats?
- ☑ Is his feeding routine consistent?
- ☑ Have you moved house?
- ☑ Have you recently introduced a new baby or other pet into the household?
- ☑ Is the home a calm place or is it noisy and unsettled?
- ☑ Is your relationship breaking down or a new one starting up?
- ☑ Is everyone in your household and extended family being consistent with him with commands, boundaries and so on?
- ☑ Does he have access to the whole house 24/7?
- ☑ Do you need to create a red zone and put up a safety gate?
- ☑ Have you moved the dog's bed?
- ☑ Have you changed your work patterns so your dog is on a different timetable now?
- ☑ Are you leaving him alone too long?
- ☑ Does he have a safe, secure place (like a crate) to call his own?
- ☑ Are his toys left out all day?

- ☑ Are you keeping your house and garden clean and clear (picking up poops and cleaning up properly after accidents)?
- ☑ Does he need desensitizing to certain noises?
- ☑ Is he getting enough mental stimulation?
- ☑ Does he have a consistent daily routine?
- ☑ Have you taught him the basic commands?
- ☑ Have you done proper dog socialization?
- ☑ Does he go to doggy day care?
- ☑ Is he getting enough physical exercise?
- ☑ Are you being clear? Does he understand what you're asking him to do?
- ☑ Have you given him a chance to do what you want him to do?
- ☑ Have you rewarded partial behaviour? Remember NILFF (Nothing in Life for Free).
- ☑ Have you gone at your dog's pace or have you rushed him?
- ☑ Do you need to muzzle or Halti train?
- ☑ Do you need a new lead?
- ☑ Are you humanizing him or thinking in terms of Pack Theory?

# CHAPTER 29

# DEALING WITH LOSS

If you have a dog, at some point you are going to have to deal with loss. None of us likes to think about it and I don't think ANYTHING can prepare you for it. It doesn't matter how old your dog is when it happens or how long they've been part of your family. IT IS HEARTBREAKING. No human being can give the love that a dog gives, it's impossible.

But after all the love and joy your dog has brought you, it's your turn to show them the final act of love and to make sure that when it's their time to go, it's done with dignity and as little pain as possible.

## Saying goodbye to Scooby

I've been DREADING revisiting this because it's still so raw talking about him, even after six years, but I think it's important. If my experience can help one person through their grief, then it will be worth it.

Scooby was seven when I noticed he had an issue with his knee. He started limping one day, so me being me, I got him in the pool for some hydrotherapy. The pool seemed to improve it a little so I thought it was his cruciate ligament. I spoke to the vet who told me to take him in for an X-ray. They called me and said, 'We don't know how to tell you this but he has a tumour and the bone in his leg is about to snap. That's why he's been limping.'

I was *reeling* with shock. I'd gone from having a fit and healthy dog with a little limp to a dog that had a terminal illness. HOW HAD THIS HAPPENED?

The vet gave me the option to have Scooby's leg amputated, which would have given us another 12 weeks but put him through major surgery with no hope of a cure because the cancer was everywhere, or I could have him put to sleep.

The cancer was all over his entire body. I couldn't put him through the pain, the operation, the recovery, just to die. Why? Because I wanted some extra time with him? That wouldn't have been fair. I didn't want to be selfish after everything he'd given me over the years. I had to do the right – awful – thing.

Don't get me wrong: if amputating his leg would have cured him, I'd have done it in a flash. With the hydrotherapy, I've worked with loads of amputees and dogs with three or even two legs can have great lives. But the cancer had spread everywhere and there was no saving him, just delaying the inevitable.

I took Scooby home for the weekend, knowing I had to take him back on Monday to have him put to sleep. It was HORRENDOUS. I kept looking at him and thinking, 'I'm sending him to his death.'

What to do with our last 48 hours together? I'd always been super strict with his diet and never let him have any human food. That weekend, I went to Marks & Spencer and I bought EVERY single item that he shouldn't have had – cream cakes, cheese, scones, everything. I wanted him to experience all those things. I sat on the kitchen floor with him and I didn't sleep for two and a half days. I fed him and hugged him and tried to savour all those last memories. His tail wagged the whole weekend.

When the time came to put him to sleep, I sat on the floor and Scooby laid across me and put his head on my leg, in a way he would never normally do, and did this big sigh.

And then he was gone.

I had no idea how his death was going to affect me, because I'd never had a dog before. No one can prepare you for the pain. It's *impossible* to describe. When you think of the worst heartbreak, it doesn't even come CLOSE to how I felt when Scooby died.

Everyone deals with their dog's death differently. Some people go straight out and get another dog, other people line up a dog before the other dog dies, and some people can't commit again. I'm in the latter camp. I haven't been able to think about getting another dog since. He's left such a scar. I'd lost my best friend, my family and my first love all in one.

## How NOT to deal with death

While there is no real right or wrong way to deal with death and grief, I definitely didn't cope well. I spiralled out of control.

Two months before I found out he had cancer, I'd moved into this lovely house with a big garden – all for Scooby. It was our little safe place but now it was EMPTY. Every time I walked through the front door or went into a room, I felt him missing. I couldn't deal with him not being there.

And rather than face up to my grief, I became a cocaine addict. I took drugs to cope. I didn't want to face normal life, so I developed an *expensive* habit. I got up each morning and had a line of coke for breakfast and then I'd take it throughout the day. At 9pm, I'd crash and go to bed.

I was having Eye Movement Desensitization and Reprocessing Therapy to deal with my childhood trauma and my therapist, Maria Cotter, told me that I needed to go to rehab or I would die. I laughed at her. I couldn't afford private rehab – it would cost a bomb! Then a friend and guardian angel, Gina Citroni, gave me the money and saved my life. If I'd have waited for National Health Service treatment, I would have been dead.

At that time, I didn't accept I was an addict. I thought my drug use was a habit I was in control of. The clinic told me to stay clean for a week before I arrived but I thought, 'No, I'll take double.'

I got on the plane to Italy three days before Christmas and was sent straight to a hospital to detox for four days. I don't remember Christmas Eve, Christmas Day or Boxing Day. Once I was completely clean, I was sent to the rehab centre – the San Nicola rehab clinic in the mountains. Maria knew that if I went somewhere in the UK I would either just walk out or have dealers passing me drugs through the windows. But this place was in the middle of nowhere. No escape.

I was so DEFIANT when I arrived. Because of the mind games my foster parents had played when I was a child, I thought the clinic staff were doing the same thing. Four weeks in, they said, 'You're not making progress, we're going to keep you in for another four weeks.' I hadn't changed at all. I was *physically* clean but mentally, my brain was EXACTLY the same.

It was all about CONTROL. They wanted me to hand control over to them. ABSOLUTELY NOT. They were asking me to give up the *very* thing that had kept me alive as a child. I COULDN'T be vulnerable. I COULDN'T let my guard down. They COULDN'T break me. To give up the thing that had protected me for so long was so hard.

Not knowing what to do, I went outside into the January cold of the mountains and sat on the edge of the hill. I looked up into the sky and said, 'Help. Please help. I need help.' I'm not religious at all but I am spiritual and I asked to be spiritually cleansed. I felt this FORCE go through me like a hurricane. I got up and walked into my first session of the morning and the counsellor looked at my face and said, 'What's just happened?' I started sobbing. I finally broke and he said, 'You're on the road to recovery now.' I accepted there was a higher power and that I had no control. That I was an addict.

For the next two weeks, they unpicked everything from my past and rewired me back properly. Rehab taught me so much about grief. It brought up feelings of loss and abandonment, which resonated with my childhood. I was mourning the first being to have ever loved me with UNCONDITIONAL love. To have felt that love and to have had it taken away was soul-destroying. Being sober and grieving you have to FACE it. There's no hiding. You have to SIT in your most uncomfortable feelings.

There was no way round it, no quick fix, no medication to block it out. If you try to avoid it, one day something will trigger that emotion, the same way it can with dogs, and that negative feeling will swamp you and you'll be right back at the start. All you've done is blocked it.

## Moving on

When I came back from rehab, I sold the big house with the garden. It didn't mean anything without Scooby to share it. It sounds weird to say but I'm so grateful for my addiction because if I hadn't gone to rehab, I would never have fixed these parts of myself. I came out of rehab the Leon that I would have been had I not suffered any childhood trauma. And it's been the most incredible journey ever since. Incredible. I have a new life. I would never have had this life if I hadn't had an addiction and gone there. That's why I'm grateful for it. I had to go through that to fix all of the stuff from the past. And not many people get the chance to do that. To live a life with nothing holding onto them. To be healed.

## Leon's 6 lessons in loss

### 1. Don't be selfish
We would all give ANYTHING for one more day, one more hour, with our loved ones but if your dog is in pain, put HIM first. I've heard people say, 'While his tail's still wagging, we'll keep him going' but dogs' tails wag even when they're in pain.

### 2. Speak to someone
It might be a friend or family member who knows what it's like to have lost a dog or it might be a professional. Avoid people who say, 'He was just a dog' and expect you to be over it in two days. You can't get over it in two days or two weeks. It's normal to feel isolated and alone in times of grief.

### 3. Don't try to block it out
We all have different coping mechanisms – over-working, medication, drinking – but try to FACE your feelings, however hard they are. In therapy, they teach you to sit with your feelings and name them rather than trying to control them. If you try to block them out now, you're simply delaying the inevitable. And you don't want a bill like mine for rehab!

### 4. Give yourself time to grieve
Your dog was never 'just' a dog, no matter what anyone else says. To you, he was part of your family. It's okay to be upset, heartbroken.

I felt like I was losing my mind but it's natural to grieve. Take however long it takes. There is no right or wrong amount of time.

### 5. Do it YOUR way
I still have Scooby's ashes and a big portrait of him on my living room wall. My plan is to bury his ashes when I find my forever home. Until then, they're on the mantelpiece. Scooby used to love lying in the sun so when the sun shines, I take the lid off the ashes and put them in the sunshine in the garden.

### 6. Do something to remember him by – but don't rush into anything
People rush to do something nice like plant a tree but once the ashes have gone, you can't get them back so take the time to make sure it's the right thing for you. Knowing my luck, I'd put them in a plant pot and the plant would die or I'd scatter them in the garden and then have to move. A friend lost his dog and he had his paw print tattooed on his arm using ink containing his ashes. That sounds freaky to some people but I think it's a lovely thing to do. You can also have ashes put into jewellery.

# CONCLUSION

Phew! I'm exhausted, I don't know about you. We've covered A LOT. We went through the basics of dog training and dog psychology so that you have a clear and full understanding of your dog, and then we looked in detail at 20 different dog challenges and how I fixed them using the simple three-step process – THE POWER OF THREE.

Throughout the case studies there were little tips and tricks as well as specific training notes for you to TRY AT HOME. I hope you found the training advice in this book easier to understand and follow than in other dog-training books and advice online.

I want you to take away ideas to build a better connection with your dog, along with training tips to help you deal with stressful issues. If you've used different techniques in the past, you might be feeling overwhelmed or guilty. You HAVE NOT messed up your dog. It's NEVER too late. And you can TOTALLY teach an old dog new tricks. You have a different way forward now. A *kind* way that actually WORKS for you *and* your dog.

The reason I love working with dogs is seeing the DIFFERENCE I make. Not only are the dogs I work with happier, but the owners are too. I watch as they *both* grow in confidence and I see the stress melt away as owners see how easy it is to fix their dog. I want the same for YOU.

I hope you've learned something; I hope I've made you laugh.

I'll leave you with the words I always say to my clients at the end of our sessions.

People say to me, 'I feel so stupid. *I've* caused this problem!' I remind them that they didn't *mean* to cause these problems and that now they know different. You can't know what you don't know.

By picking up this book, you've reached out for help. And that is to be applauded. There are so many incorrect or misleading myths about how to train your dog ingrained in our society and hopefully this book has explained the TRUTH.

Now you know *different*. Go and nurture a wonderful relationship with your dog built on mutual TRUST and RESPECT and don't forget that he has a VOICE too.

Love Leon x

# ACKNOWLEDGEMENTS

Thank you to Trevor Davies, Rimsha Falak, Rosa Patel and Charlotte Sanders at Octopus Publishing Group, for believing in me and helping me get this book out in the world.

Throughout my life I have been blessed with guardian angels, parental figures who helped save me time and time again after my father died and I was taken away from my birth mother. Without those people, I wouldn't be here today.

Each of them came into my life right at the point I needed them the most. These guardian angels have guided me and cared for me at different times of my life. They've all been as special as each other. I want to thank them for keeping me alive and getting me to where I am now. They each took a block and built me up, gave me confidence, and laid the foundations for who I am today. They still support and guide me. None of them has ever left my life and that's incredibly beautiful.

After I was taken away from my birth mother, my foster sister, Janice Fryer, was the first maternal figure in my life. I just ADORED her. She was older and she'd come home from school and make a fuss of me as a toddler.

When I was 14, Pam Deans was the social worker who saved me and took me away from my foster parents. She was my guardian angel until I was in my twenties.

My foster auntie, Marion Bertouche, supported me when I went into the care system after I left my foster parents. She let me stay at hers on the weekends. The children's home was like a remand centre and she hated that I was there.

When I was 23, foster aunt and uncle, Jackie and Jim Vance, took me in, saved me, showed me the REAL meaning of parents after I'd had mental health issues.

When I went to college to study drama aged 24, there was a lecturer called Steve Dolan who gave me the courage and determination to write and express myself. He gave me lots of parental love and guidance. He told me I was special and talented and his words of encouragement still stay with me today. He brought me out of my shell and gave me the freedom to express myself.

Jan and John Henderson were like my parents from the age of 24 to 36. In fact, I called Jan 'Mum'.

Angela Griffiths at Greyfriars helped me completely change path to hydrotherapy. She believed in me, gave me encouragement, trusted my judgement and I flourished under her guidance.

Gina Citroni became a client at my doggy day care business and a true friend. She saved my life by paying for me to go to rehab and kept my business going for three years. She paid the staff's wages, gave me support, gave me her team of people. She was like a business angel AND mum figure. She is just AMAZING.

Carla and Roberto, with whom I have shared 24 years of tears and laughter. My love for you and the unwavering support you have provided me is immeasurable. I am so grateful that I now have the opportunity to give back some of that support, and I am SO proud of you and what you have achieved with your sensational pet brand – Paw Originals, Glasgow.

Maria Cotter was my EMDR therapist who put me on the path to rehab and gave me a whole new lease of life.

Andrew Harvey, who set me back on my spiritual path, helped me become more self-aware and taught me how to resonate on a higher frequency. Thanks to you, four years ago, I became vegan literally overnight!

I met Nick Fraser and Clive Fisher in a Glasgow nightclub 20 years ago; they took me in when I was homeless. I came out of rehab and with their strength and support, I started a new life.

My 24-year friendship with Ian McLeod: he is a true friend and has supported me over the years as a strong pillar and foundation of my life.

Kirsty Milner, who has been a HUGE part of my life for the last four years. Thank you, from the bottom of my heart, for helping me evolve and for making this book possible!

And then I was reunited with my birth mum, Audrey, when I came out of rehab. It was the most incredible, beautiful feeling.

My PR team, my very own Charlie's Angels at Siren Talent: Grainne, Sarah, Kate. They're absolute POWERHOUSES.

Thank you to Scooby for teaching me how to love and be loved.

Thank you to Dean Bailey, my partner, my twin flame. He truly is mine. I have the most amazing life with you.

Thank you to all my wonderful clients who trust me with their dogs. And thank you to the dogs for teaching me so much more than I ever taught you.

Finally, a *massive* thank you to YOU.

# INDEX

# ABOUT THE AUTHOR

Leon Towers is a qualified dog behaviourist, nutritionist and hydrotherapist, who has spent the last 12 years improving the lives of over 16,000 dogs. He reported on Crufts in 2019 and is the host for Channel 4's hit shows *Embarrassing Pets* and *My Gay Dog*. *Meet the PAW-rents: Celebrities and Their Dogs* is his latest project with Channel 5.

Leon does one-to-one private home visits designed to assist individuals and their families in gaining confidence in addressing their dog's behavioural issues.

For more information about Leon and his services, please visit: www.leontowers.co.uk or email leon.towers@hotmail.com.

Instagram: @leontowersthedogsvoice and @thelodgedogdaycare

Facebook: The Lodge Dog Daycare with Leon & Dean